Copyright

Although the author and publisher have made eve this book was correct at press time, the author and publi(s) any liability to any party for any loss, damage, or disrupti(on) such errors or omissions result from negligence, accident, or any other cause.

Copying, publishing, distributing, using and/or forwarding the content to others or in other media is not allowed and is considered a violation of copyright and punishable by law. If you wish to use content do contact the author.

Author and publisher cannot be held responsible or liable in any way whatsoever for and/or in connection with any consequences and/or damage resulting from the proper, complete and timely dispatch and receipt of the content.

With gratitude

Cover Illustration Painting of Mary Magdalene by Marie-France Lebailly.

Book design by Abraham Tol - www.atol-solutions.com

Author Jaap Rameijer

Photographs Jaap Rameijer

Contents

PREFACE 5

INTRODUCTION 6

WHO WAS MARY MAGDALENE? 17

JESUS AND MARY MAGDALENE 21

THE CRUCIFIXION 29

HER FLIGHT TO FRANCE 31

WHERE DID SHE PREACH 42

LA SAINTE BAUME 51

RENNES-LE-CHÂTEAU 57

HER FINAL RESTING PLACE 67

JOSEPH OF ARIMATHEA 71

THE DESPOSYNI 77

BLACKENING THE NAME OF MARY MAGDALENE 83

THE POWER OF THE CHURCH 87

THE KNIGHTS TEMPLAR 103

THE HOLY GRAIL 113

BLACK MADONNA'S 119

FAMOUS FACES AND SCENES 137

    Royal/regal 144

    Repenting/pensive 149

    Sorrow/despair 152

    Standing or sitting at the cross 158

    Taken off the cross 163

    "Damaged" pictures 166

    Noli mi Tangere 168

    Boat Pictures 170

    Pregnant 170

HER LOVE FOR JESUS 173

SACRED FEMININITY 179

THE SECOND HOLY COUNTRY 187

A PILGRIMAGE 193

A MESSAGE TO THE CHURCH 209

EPILOGUE 213

BIBLIOGRAPHY	215
About Jaap Rameijer	217
Books by Jaap Rameijer	218

PREFACE

As a young boy I dreamed a lot.

From time to time I traveled back in time and cruised the Universe. I was in Atlantis. I was there when the Pyramids were built. At the time it all seemed quite normal to me. I enjoyed the views of other worlds. Others thought my dreams strange, unusual. They didn't have dreams like that.

But there was still something missing. I didn't know what, but I did know that an important period in my life was missing. Then the dreams disappeared. I had suppressed them.

Later my school, my friends and the "roaring sixties" occupied my mind. And then, my work. I was a professional naval officer for almost 20 years. I got married and had three children. I finished master studies in law and business management. I left the Navy and got new jobs, tough jobs. With Fokker, aircraft manufacturer. As managing director of a health insurance company. As director of a group of psychiatric hospitals. As vice chairman of a university. Important jobs, but not always nice jobs. High status and good salary, yes, but the jobs also carried heavy responsibilities.

What bothered me most was that I had to act, often, against my feelings. Leading painful reorganizations, firing people. It drove me to the brink of a burnout. A burnout is, in my view, not so much caused by stress, or working too hard, but by working against your heart, your feelings. Next comes the midlife crisis, with questions as "who am I" and "what am I doing here?" Followed by "do I want to do this for the rest of my life?" And "what have I contributed to mankind". And "what is really important to me?"

Mary Magdalene

My life changed. Health, family, friendship, love and doing good work became more important than work, money and status. It was a spiritual awakening. My dreams came back. Then I read the bestseller the *"Holy Blood and the Holy Grail"* by Baigent, Leigh and Lincoln. It was as if a door opened in my mind. Mary Magdalene came through that door.

The "real" Mary Magdalene. Not the repentant sinner of the Church, but the beautiful and powerful consort of Jesus. Mary Magdalene came back in my life. And then I knew what had been missing in my dreams.

In 1998 a well-known medium channeled Mary Magdalene for me. It was one of the most moving experiences in my life. Mary welcomed me like a lost brother. "I am so happy to see you again," she said. She told me that 2,000 years ago I had lived in the area of Rennes-le-Château. I knew all the rivers, rocks, trees, springs, caves, elf's, gnomes and spirits of the place. And I waited for something to happen, for someone to come. I didn't know who or what. But when Mary Magdalene came to this area, I knew. It was she that I had been waiting for. I became her guide, her protector and her messenger boy. She "told" me, through this medium, that we often sat for hours in her cave, talking, meditating and dreaming. I adored her. What a wonderful woman she was. When Mary Magdalene "spoke" to me, the tears ran down my cheeks. I recognized my past life. She said that I had died quite young and that she was not allowed to save me.

Then she told me that I had promised, in this life, to tell the truth about her. To tell the world who she really was. The way I saw her. It was to be her story and my story. The story of the woman I loved.

The story of the woman who loves us all.

Cave of Mary Magdalene Rennes-le-Château

6

INTRODUCTION

Once you have been there, you are hooked; you are "lost." You won't be able to forget it. It is so special, so wonderful and so lovely. It has a great impact on people. It triggers old memories. You know that you have been there before. You can feel it, in your bones, in your heart. You are happy, very happy and sometimes you are sad. You look in wonder around you. And when you leave, you know that one day you will be back.

This is what happens to people visiting the sacred places of the world. Like Mount Shasta in the USA, Palenque in Mexico, Machu Picchu in Peru, Anghor Wak in Cambodia, the Borobudur in Indonesia, Glastonbury in England, Rennes-le-Château in France and many other places in India, Tibet, Nepal and the rest of the world.

What is it? What is happening? Is it the energy? Are previous lives coming to the surface, to our conscious mind? Is our collective memory triggered? Are we being directed or guided by "The Great Nautonnier," the "One" up there who "controls" our lives. Did He tell us to come to these sacred places? Are we meant to find our destiny there? Or do we go there to be healed or "energized"?

Rennes-le-Château

I don't know, but this is what happened to me when I first came to Rennes-le-Château.

I had just read the book *"The Holy Blood and the Holy Grail"*. It was like a revelation. This I understood, this sounded plausible. Many things in the Bible that I did not understand, or found hard to believe, suddenly fell into place. Here a different scenario was presented. Here the historical Jesus and Mary Magdalene were presented, not the biblical ones and certainly not what the Church had made of them. The customs and culture in Palestine, 2000 years ago, were described. A lot of attention was given to how the Bible was brought about. How this "Holy" book came into being. And how the power plays of popes, emperors, kings and cardinals had shaped the Church. It was very different from what the Church wanted us to believe. And there was Mary Magdalene. Not a sinner, but a wonderful woman, a wealthy and very spiritual woman.

In 1995 my wife Joke (Joanna) and I were on holiday in France and Spain. We first visited Lourdes. And who knows, maybe we got some inspiration there. Then we went to Andorra, the little mountain state in the Pyrenees. There I realized that we were quite close to the "Pays Cathare", the Cathar country. So we traveled to the magical 'Pays Cathare' and immediately things began to happen. Strange things. Pure synchronicity.

Montaillou

My first Cathar castle was Montaillou. Known from the book *"Montaillou"* by Emmanuel Le Roy Ladurie. It is not a very impressive ruin, not at all, but I got terribly exited. Running around, looking everywhere, touching stones and shouting "look at this" and "look at that." I don't know why I behaved like that, it just happened.

My next castle was Puivert, the castle of the Troubadours and of courtly love. It was after 1700 hours and the castle was closed. But I had to get in. I just had to. So I climbed the walls, a pretty dangerous job. I stayed inside for over half an hour. When I came out my wife was furious. Worried stiff that something had happened to me. She even threw her stick at me!

Chateau Puivert

Asmodeus Rennes-le-Château

The next day we went to Rennes-le-Château. There again all kinds of strange things happened. The church, dedicated to Mary Magdalene in 1059, with the original statue of Asmodeus, the keeper of secrets, gave me the creeps. In 1996 an unknown vandal cut off his head. It has been replaced. It was the fourth time that statues had been stolen from the church or damaged by vandals, the Mayor told me. But after a while this church began to fascinate me. With all its curious paintings, statues, stained glass windows and inscriptions. And the strange lay-out of the place.

Out on the street I ran into an elderly Englishman, Graham Simmans, writer and amateur archeologist. We talked for hours about Jesus, Mary Magdalene, their children and their life in Egypt. It was incredible. Talking with a complete stranger about such sensitive topics in the street of Rennes-le-Château. Later on we became good friends. He wrote two books about this subject, *"Rex Deus"* and just before he died *"Jesus after the Crucifixion"*.

Rennes-le-Château

Back home in the Netherlands I realized that something important had happened. For it was impossible to forget Rennes-le-Château. The place had gotten under my skin, in my blood, in my bones. I had to go back. And I did. So during the following years we came back to Rennes-le-Château. Sometimes six times a year.

I had a tough job then, well paid but full of stress. I was regularly on the verge of a burnout. When I got into the danger zone I told my secretary that I would take the day off on Friday. And drove, in one day, over 1300 km's to Rennes-le-Château, where I stayed for a day. On Saturday sniffing around, visiting "old" places, talking with friends, walking the beautiful land, enjoying the good food, the wine and the company of other people. Then, on Sunday I drove back to the Netherlands, happy and fully "charged". "Energized" might be a better word. Now I could cope with my job for another three to four months.

But it did not stop there. We came so often to Rennes-le-Château that we thought it might be a good idea to buy a small holiday home in the area. Prices were still reasonable then. But there was nothing for sale. Then Graham Simmans mentioned the "Les Labadous". A domain consisting of three big buildings, on 8,000 square meters of land. Situated one kilometer south of Rennes-le-Château, in a beautiful valley, next to a stream called the River of Colors; bordered by huge, black poplar trees. But far too big for a holiday home.

However, the moment we saw the property, we knew. Both of us knew. This was it. This was our destiny. This was the place we had to buy. But Les Labadous was in a horrible state. Originally built as a spiritual center by the writer Elizabeth van Buren, it had changed hands a few times and was now occupied by a woman who also wanted to make it into a spiritual center. But she did not succeed. Now it housed stray dogs, about 35 of them, dangerous and dirty. Nobody dared to come close. But still

Les Labadous Rennes-le-Château

when we saw the place, even though it was in such a sad state, we knew: "this is it". This is the place meant for us. Clear as crystal. This is our destiny.

But could we buy it? We had no money, three children going to university, aging parents and a stiff mortgage on our present house. Then synchronicity took over. Even now I still can't fully comprehend what happened in that period. The children finished their studies, our parents moved to old people's homes, I got fired with a golden handshake and we could sell our house for a good price. Just before Christmas 1998 we were able to buy Les Labadous. My wife moved in on January 4th 1999, while I stayed in Holland, earning money for the necessary repairs and renovations. Joke stayed at Les Labadous. And made it into a beautiful "Chambres d'Hotes and Gites".

During the past 14 years we have received thousands of guests. Friends, spiritual groups, writers, researchers, journalists, scientists, camera teams, people with special skills, adventurers, all kinds of people. They came from all over the world. Mostly from Europe, but also from Canada, New Zealand, Peru and Japan. The last couple of years more people came from the USA. Several seminars were held at our place. Sound healing sessions, crystal skull ceremonies and Tantra healings. Wonderful festivities took place, like wedding

Mary Magdalene silhouetted in the tree at Les Labadous

parties or music festivals. Les Labadous grew into a well-known, spiritual place, endowed with a wonderful energy. The energy of Mary Magdalene, a powerful healing, creative and loving energy. From 1998 onwards I became more and more interested in Mary Magdalene. I went to all the places in France where she is honored and remembered, where she is still "alive". Where her presence and energy is still felt. Places where the people still remember her and love her. I went to caves, springs, sources, chapels, abbeys, churches, basilicas, and cathedrals, all over France. Tracing her footsteps, feeling her energy. And taking the most wonderful pictures of her beautiful face. I came back to Mary Magdalene and she came back to me. Showing herself in the bark of one of the big black poplar trees at Les Labadous.

I also became interested in Black Virgins or Black Madonna's. I felt that they were closely related to Mary Magdalene. Representing the Mother Goddess, Mother Earth. Representing ancient, powerful, female Goddesses. Their creative power, their power to destruct. Their healing power, their wisdom, their love. I found that Black Madonna's and Mary Magdalene are often present at the same site. And at sacred places. Old sacred places of the druids. In wells, caves, on mountain sides. Spots were streams, energy lines or ley lines intersect. Some Black Madonna's were very ancient, dating from pre Christian times. Many were found at curious places, in trees, caves or even arriving in open boats. Simple, poor people often found them, like shepherds, farmers and fishermen. These statues have enormous power. When we see them we are always somewhat taken aback and fascinated. The common people adore them. The statues are often an embarrassment to the Church, which is, I think, more of a good sign, than a bad sign

Now I live permanently at Les Labadous. It is the most beautiful place in France. Situated in the commune of Rennes-le-Château, that mysterious mountain village at the foot of the Pyrenees. Les Labadous is a sacred place. In fact, the whole area around Rennes-le-Château is sacred, including Alet-les-Bains, Arques, Bugarach, Rennes-les-Bains and Campagne-les-Bains. "Les Labadous" means the washing place, the cleansing place in Occitan language. It is a place where people can still feel the presence and the energy of Mary Magdalene.

My interest in Rennes-le-Château and in Mary Magdalene increased year by year. I thoroughly researched the area. On foot with my faithful dog, a Rhodesian ridgeback called "Mayday". Or by car, visiting all the interesting places of the area. In the Pays Cathare and far beyond it. In the whole south of France. Following in the footsteps of Mary Magdalene, the Visigoths, the Merovingian's, the Carolingians, the Cathars and the Knights Templar. I read hundreds of books on these topics and followed up many interesting leads. I spoke to writers, researchers, camera teams, local experts, spiritual groups and psychics. And I am a member of various organizations researching the mysteries of Rennes-le-Château.

I also got involved in "spiritual" matters. Feeling myself being directed to certain places. Feeling the "need" to investigate and research certain items. But I kept my feet on the ground. After all I served almost 20 years in the Royal Netherlands Navy and I have Masters' degrees both in Law and in Business Management. So I am firmly "grounded", I dare say.

I became interested in esoteric topics. I took training courses in Reiki, curing illnesses with my hand and using strange symbols. I did channeling courses, learning how to act as a medium for masters, guides, or whoever is "living" up there, in the Other World. I met many psychics, people who could communicate with other entities, like masters, angels, guides, or with deceased persons. I got many readings, where psychic people contacted "entities from the other world", entities that had important messages for me. I did regression therapies, going back in time and experiencing past lives. I was regularly "updated" by astrologists, telling me about possible paths for the future. I followed spiritual courses like

Basilica of St. Maximin

Tantra, and sound healing. I practiced meditation, Yoga and more, much more. And I can say, cross my heart, that there are indeed other worlds, other dimensions, and other energies. There is more out there than meets the eye.

In the past years I guided several groups and individuals in the south of France, mainly in the area around Rennes-le-Château and in the Pays Cathare. But also far east, as far as St-Maximin-La-Ste-Baume, 50 km's east of Aix-en-Provence, the place where Mary Magdalene is supposed to be buried, or far west, to Toulouse, Foix and Pamiers.

Always following in the footsteps of Mary Magdalene, the Cathars and the Knights Templar. Learning new things and gaining new insights. But the most important source of information was living here. Listening to the people of the land. Talking with writers, researches, journalists. And participating in channeling sessions, readings and shared visions.

Stronghold Montségur

Most of my information however comes from the "Pays Cathare". Where I visited the places where Mary Magdalene is still honored. I think that I went more than 90 times to the Cave of Mary Magdalene, close to Les Labadous. And climbed over 60 times the Cathar stronghold of Montségur. I visited many other places in France and in Catalonia in north-east Spain. Places where the "presence" of Mary Magdalene is also strongly felt. And places where famous Black Madonna's are venerated.

I have written three books, in Dutch, my mother language, about the Secret Messages of Rennes-le-Château. Paying special attention to Berenger Saunière, the "million dollar priest" who stayed in Rennes-le-Château from 1885 to his death in 1917. He renovated and decorated the little church dedicated to Mary Magdalene. It now harbors 96 anomalies of what is normal in a small parish church in the south of France. He also built the Villa Bethania and the Tour Magdala. His whole life was dedicated to Mary Magdalene. And more than 600 books have been written about his life and his enigmatic church.

But we still we don't know what his secret was, or where he got his money from.

Tour Magdala *Villa Bethania*

I also wrote a book about Glastonbury, another Holy Place in Europe, closely related to Rennes-le-Château. It is titled *"Glastonbury and the Holy Grail"*, written in Dutch.

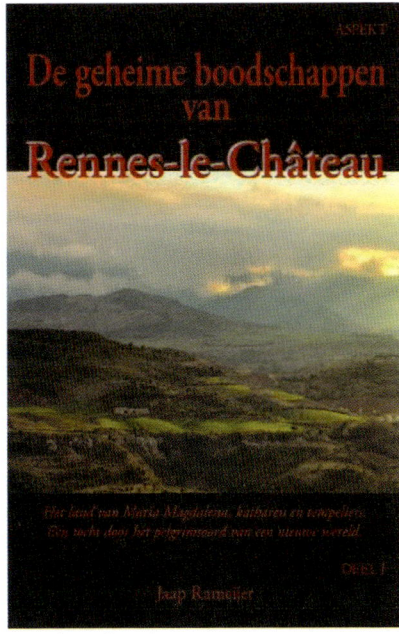

My first book *Glastonbury*

Now it is time for a new book, about Mary Magdalene. Celebrating the "revival" of this extraordinary woman. About "Mary Magdalene in France", which I see as the Second Holy Country. It is a simple book. Written from the head and the heart. With lots of pictures. Pictures that say more than words. Pictures of Mary Magdalene, of Black Madonna's and of sacred sites. With short paragraphs of supporting text.

Anna and Mary

It is about a woman and her religion, the original teachings of Jesus and Mary Magdalene. It is about a special country, France.

It is about the historical Jesus and Mary Magdalene, about his nephew John the Baptist and his brother Joseph of Arimathea.

It is about Jesus' grandmother Anne and his mother Mary. It is about their bloodlines. And the blackening of Mary Magdalene and with her all women, by the Church of Rome. It is about the Cathars and the Knights Templar, about sacred femininity and about the Church of Rome. And it is about the now.

It is about the revival of Mary Magdalene and sacred femininity. And the downfall of the Church. For now Mary Magdalene is "alive". Revived by bestsellers as *"The Holy Blood and the Holy Grail"* and *"The Da Vinci Code"*. Now people want to know more about her. There are many questions. Who was she? Where did she live in Palestine, the first Holy Land? What was her relationship with Jesus? Why did she flee to France, the Second Holy Land? Did Jesus have brothers and sisters? Did Jesus and Mary have children? Where did she go or where did they go? Where did they live and preach in France. What did Mary Magdalene do? What happened to her offspring, the Desposyni? There are many, many stories about all these topics, written by scientific researchers, biblical scholars, and church officials. There are channeled books or books from people having visions. My book is a book from the mind and the heart. I visited all the places where Mary Magdalene went. And I live in such a place. I experienced and experience every day the wonderful energy of Mary Magdalene. And I tell my story with pictures. Pictures that say more than a thousand words.

There are many questions related to Mary Magdalene. For example: what is Catharism, the religion of the Cathars? Is it a Gnostic religion? Was it based on the original teachings of Jesus and Mary Magdalene? Or even older than that? What have the Roman emperors and the popes done to Christianity? Did they make it into a state religion, a power tool?

What have they done to Mary Magdalene and to women in general? And why? Were they scared? What was her relationship with the Knights Templar? What secrets did they possess? And why were they so fiercely protecting Mary Magdalene and John the Baptist? I cannot answer all those questions. Many books, scientific books, have been written about these topics. But I can provide you with stories, various stories, the most interesting stories, but still stories, for there is, up till now, not one simple truth. My stories come from the heart, stories that tell a likely scenario. Then it will be up to you to choose and decide what to believe.

Mary Magdalene, Savior of the Church

And last but not least, what is happening now? Do we see a revival, a "resurrection" of Mary Magdalene? The rise of sacred femininity? A revival of Gnostic Christianity? Is she the woman who might save the Church? The apostle of the apostles. And would she want to save the Church? The Church of Rome and all the other churches, catholic or protestant. Mary Magdalene, the "Savior of the Church". That would be something, wouldn't it?

WHO WAS MARY MAGDALENE?

Mary Magdalene was a special woman. She was no prostitute, but a woman of high birth. Some say she was a princess, or high priestess from Egypt, Ethiopia or Syria. Others say she had royal blood in her lineage. There are stories that she had a dark skin and stories that she had a lighter skin than usual. Some say that Mary Magdalene belonged to the lost tribe of Benjamin. Others say she was a descendant from the queen of Sheba. We just don't know.

According to Laurence Gardner, whom I consider to be the most authoritative writer and researcher on Mary Magdalene, she was born in 3 AD. As the daughter of Mattheus Syro Jairus, a nobleman from Syria, first priest among the high priests of Jerusalem and Eucharia who descended from the Hasmonese house of the Macabees. Mary Magdalene did not come from Magdala, as many think, but most likely from Capernaum. She was called: Mary "The Magdalen" which meant Mary the Tower, or Mary the Castle, Mary the Exalted. Magdala was a title, an addition that signaled a high social status. And she was rich. Here she is drawn as a young woman.

A portrait made for me by Ingrid Riedel

Mary Magdalene is named several times in the Bible. And contrary to what many may think, not in a bad way at all. She is almost always mentioned first of all the women who travel with Jesus. As the woman who is at the crucifixion, with his mother and sisters. As the woman, who is the first to meet Jesus at the open tomb, taking him for a gardener. And on several other occasions.

During the first centuries AD Mary Magdalene was widely honored and respected; in Palestine, Egypt, France and Great Britain. She was the "Apostle of the Apostles". She was the woman who had it all, the beauty, the wisdom, the compassion, the suffering, and the love. She was, in my words, a "Total Woman". She had all a woman, or man, could wish for. She was also a woman to whom people could relate, especially women. And who men loved and respected. She was the high priestess who initiated Jesus in the mysteries of Egypt, she was the Goddess of love and creation, the Queen and the bride who anointed him and made him King. And activated this Christ consciousness.

Mary Magdalene is firmly embedded in de minds and hearts of the French people. Despite the hostility of the early church fathers towards women. Despite the systematic vilification by the Church. Despite the terrible persecutions of the Desposyni, her bloodline. Despite the murderous Albigensian crusade against the Cathars and the disbanding of the Knights Templar. Despite the horrible Inquisition and the fierce religious wars with the

Huguenots. Despite the shameful persecution of witches in the past centuries. And despite the horrors of the French Revolution. She was and still is lovingly remembered in France. Because she is a special woman. A woman who touched the hearts of the common people. Who gave them love, wisdom and hope, a woman with compassion. And a very pious woman.

She was never forgotten. Because she preached a wonderful message. Because she was the embodiment of the Mother Goddess. Because she cared for mankind. Because many royal dynasties were, and still are, proud of their, reputed descent from Jesus and Mary Magdalene. Or from Joseph of Arimathea and the English princes Enygeusa (see chapter 9). Dynasties that was not afraid to say so. Clear "proof", in my mind that they knew that Jesus and Mary Magdalene were married and had children. Among them King Clovis I, the powerful King of the Franks, who belonged to the dynasty of the famous Merovingian's.

Clovis, who was baptized in Reims in 496 AD. The place where since that time all Kings of France were crowned. He visited the tomb of Mary Magdalene in St-Maximin-Ste-Baume as early as 500 AD. Thus "proving" that Mary Magdalene had indeed sailed from Palestine or Egypt, to France.

Clovis Baptized

The crypte in St. Maximin

Since then hundreds of kings, dukes, princes and counts, and even popes, have visited her tomb in the crypt of the basilica of St-Maximin-Ste-Baume. See chapter 6.

And the abbots, monks and scribes in the abbeys, cloisters and monasteries, servants of God who were not under the direct control of Rome, they too had a special regard for Mary Magdalene. Think for example of one of the most famous and most powerful monks of France, Bernard de Clairvaux. Who compared her with the queen of Sheba, the woman so dearly loved by King Solomon. The love that was recorded, in the beautiful *"Song of Songs"*. This abbot was so charmed by Mary Magdalene that he made the Knights Templar at their initiation swear an oath of loyalty to the House of Bethany, the house of Mary Magdalene, Martha and Lazarus. Later in the 12th century AD all the churches and cathedrals that were built with money from the Knights Templar, were originally dedicated to Mary Magdalene. And many of the oldest churches in France were also, originally, dedicated to Mary Magdalene, like the churches in Rennes-le-Château, St Maximin-la-Ste-Baume, Troyes, Aix-en-Provence and Vezelay. Later the Church changed Mary Magdalene "labels" back to Virgin Mary labels.

Church of St. Victor

Mary Magdalene is supposed to have died in 63 AD. Where she is buried, no one knows. Probably some of her bones rest in an alabaster tomb in the vault of the basilica of St-Maximin-la-Ste-Baume, 50 kilometers east of Aix-en-Provence. This tomb was guarded by the Cassianite monks. Another indication that "proved" that Mary Magdalene had come to France.

Jean Cassian or Cassianus, founded the Cassianite order in 410 AD. He was one of the monks of the basilica of St. Victor in Marseille. He also founded the first cloister. A religious society that operated more or less independent from the Church. From him stem the famous words: "monks should, at all costs, avoid bishops". How true, how very true.

It may sound strange, but the Catholic Church formally reinstated Mary Magdalene in 1969. Only then was she "officially" canonized. Before that time she was, officially, considered to be a sinner, doing penitence. Her feast day, as a saint, became the 22nd of July, a date that was already in use since the 8th century. The reason for her new "canonical status" was that she had done penitence long enough. But nobody said for what.

King Clovis - Chapel ND de Bethleem, Ferrieres

Clothilde - Chapel ND de Bethleem, Ferrieres

JESUS AND MARY MAGDALENE

Jesus really existed. Some people have doubted this, but during the last decennia so many documents surfaced mentioning Jesus, or Christ, or the heir from the House of David, that we cannot doubt his existence any more. There is even a story about a document written by Jesus himself. See the book: *"The Jesus Papers, Exposing the Greatest Cover-Up in History"* by Michael Baigent.

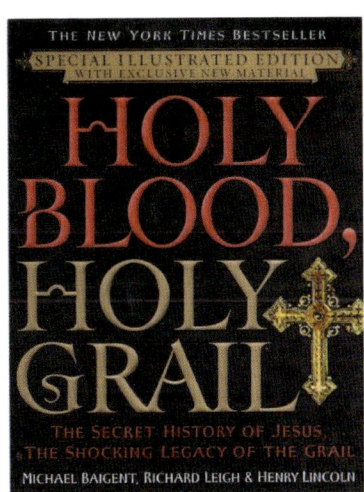

During the last decennia many books appeared about the historical Jesus and Mary Magdalene. Not the biblical Jesus and Mary, but the historical Jesus and Mary. Some are exciting novels like the books of Kathleen McGowan, called *"The expected One"* and *"The book of Love"*. Some are partly novel, partly research, such as the bestsellers *"The Holy Blood and the Holy Grail"* and *"The Da Vinci Code"*.

Other books are the result of more detailed, scientific research. Like the books written by Lynn Picknett and Clive Prince, Graham Phillips, Margaret Starbird, Susan Haskins, Elaine Pagels, Christian Doumerge, Karen Armstrong and Laurence Gardner. And then there are the channeled books, written by a medium or books resulting from visions. Some of them contain interesting stories and are very moving, like *"The Magdalen Manuscript"* by Tom Kenyon and Judi Sion, *"I remember Union"*, by Flo Aeveia Magdalena and *"The Two Mary's"* by Sylvia Browne.

According to Laurence Gardner Jesus was born on Sunday 1st of March in the year 7 BC. I know it sounds a bit strange that Jesus was born 7 years "Before Christ", but that's how it is. His mother Mary was a special woman. She was married to Joachim, also named Joseph, which was an honorary title. The mother of Mary, Anna, was also special. These two women, Anna and her daughter Mary, are very popular in France. Nearly every church has a statue of Anna with child. Recently several books appeared, most of them channeled books, about them. Such as "Anna, the grandmother of Jesus" by Claire Heartsong. A mind blowing combination of love, suffering, high spirituality and sophisticated technology.

There are many stories about Jesus and Mary Magdalene. They shouldn't or couldn't be married, according to the Roman Catholic Church, the Church that didn't exist at that time. But it is highly improbable that they were not married. A Jewish man and certainly a rabbi and most certainly a successor from the line of David, had to be married. And quite recently a document written in Coptic was discovered by Karen King, professor of Theology at Harvard University with the text "Jesus said to them, my wife…" Another indication that Jesus was married.

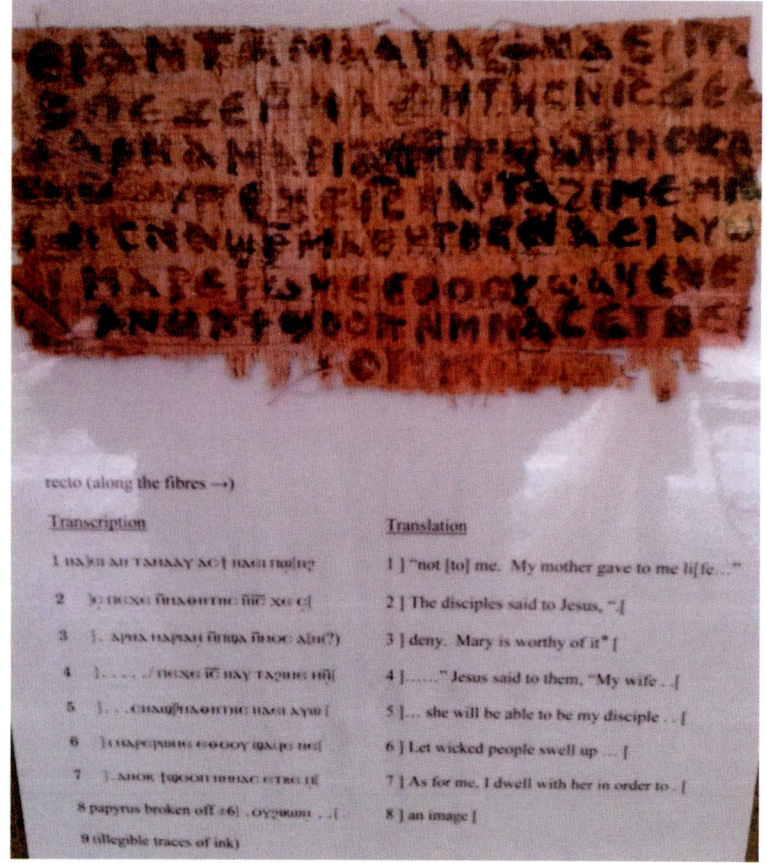

... Jesus said to them, my wife...

Now we have a much better picture of Jesus and Mary Magdalene. The historical Jesus and Mary Magdalene. Thanks to the discovery at the end 18th century of the Pistis Sophia documents.

Qumran

And the discovery in 1945 of the Nag Hammadi parchments, 13 books bound in leather with 52 texts, buried in the sands of southern Egypt. And the discovery of the Dead Sea Scrolls in 1947 in Qumran, with more discoveries during the following years.

And thanks to the discovery of the Gospel of Judas, that only recently was translated. Giving us a totally different view of Judas and his relationship with Jesus. Thanks to the discovery of these books, parchments and scrolls, we now know much more about the historical Jesus and Mary Magdalene and the culture and customs of that era, then before.

A map of the Holy Land during the time of Christ

In my view many more books, scrolls, parchments and papers are waiting to be discovered. Buried deep in the archives of universities, abbeys, churches and even the Vatican. Or under the sand and in the caves of the deserts of the Middle East. Or in private collections. And most certainly in the shops and stores of cunning Arab merchants, who are waiting for the right time to present their treasures. And who knows, some important documents may even be buried here, in the South of France, where several other treasures are also waiting to be discovered.

And let us also not forget the benefits of modern technology. Now extensive excavations are carried out in the Middle East, using the best techniques available. Dating of artifacts is easily done using C-14 dating methods. Reliable information is coming from the DNA-strings and the genes of long dead people. Tracing their race and origin. Serious studies are performed of handwriting, semantics, culture and customs of that era. The ancient religions of Egypt, Sumer and India are studied, religions that had a major influence on Christianity. As well as contemporary religions like Zaraotoisms and the Sun God. Other Christian religions are scrutinized, like the Aryanism, Coptic, Russian and Greek orthodox religions, as well as Mandaeism, which is still practiced by the followers of John the Baptist in South-Iraq. And of course the wonderful Gnostic religions like Catharism and the teachings of the Celtic church. We know more, much more today about the times of Jesus, then a hundred years ago.

Mary Magdalene was married to Jesus in the year 30 AD and again in the year 33 AD. That sounds a bit strange, but I will explain. Dynastic marriages followed a strict procedure, consisting of different phases. First the betrothal in June 30 AD. That was the well-known engagement party in Canaan, where Jesus transformed water into wine. Some beautiful pictures of Jesus proposing to Mary Magdalene can be seen in the church of St. Martin in Limoux.

Jesus "proposing" to Mary - Church of St. Martin

Enlarged Jesus "proposing" to Mary - Church of St. Martin

Although it has been argued here that Jesus might be raising Jairus' daughter from the dead. But Jairus' daughter is Mary Magdalene! And I am captivated by the secret smile on the face of that beautiful woman.

24

After that came the official wedding party in September, the month of atonement, in the house of Simon, where Mary Magdalene is sitting at Jesus feet, shedding tears and drying his feet with her hair. After which she anointed him with fragrant oil from an alabaster jar.

Maria Magdalena at Jesus feet, Rennes-le-Château

Finally the consummation of the marriage. Intimate relations were allowed in December, in order to give birth to the child in September, the month of Atonement. If the woman didn't get pregnant then intimate relations could not resume before the next December. No easy task I would think. But the laws for dynastic marriages were very strict in that time. Mary Magdalene finally gets pregnant in December 32 AD. And here a strange phenomenon occurs. There are several pictures of a pregnant Maries in France, such as here in Aigues Mortes, but also in Cucugnan, the famous "Marie Enceinte".

Pregnant Mary in Aigues Mortes　　　　　　　　　　*"Marie Enceinte" in Cucugnan*

In this church you will also find is a nice collection of pictures of pregnant Maries, from all over France. Obviously meant to prove that this pregnant Mary is the Virgin Mary. But that does not ring true. Somehow the Virgin Mary and visible pregnancy don't go together.

Therefore I think that we can safely presume that it is Mary Magdalene that is portrayed here. Isn't it funny that when the Church really wants to "promote" or impose her version of a story, it is often done so excessively, so "overdone", that it only proves the opposite. Besides her loose hair and also the local folktales, all support the notion that it is Mary Magdalene. See chapter 17.

But even if women are pregnant things are not certain. After all a miscarriage can still occur. So the next ceremony is held when she is 3 months pregnant. That was in March 33 AD in the house of Simon-Lazarus. There Mary Magdalene anoints Jesus with the precious Nardus oil, an extract from a rare plant growing in the Himalayas at an altitude above 4500 meters. She pours the oil over his head and his feet, following an age-old ritual. A ritual reserved exclusively for the bride. It was both an initiation, Jesus now became "The Anointed One", the Messiah and a confirmation of the marriage, the Holy Marriage, the "Hieros Gamos". You can read this story in the New Testament, but again in veiled terms.

In fact most of the information about the Holy Family was written in a symbolic language, so as not to alert the Romans. Symbolic numbers and gematria were widely used in the sacred texts. Gematria is the science where the sum of certain letters and phrases produced sacred numbers. See the book *"Magdalene's Lost Legacy"* by Margaret Starbird and *"The Bible's Hidden Cosmology"* by Gordon Strachan. Much of this symbolic language was later taken literally, leading to some of the most incredible "explanations" by the church. Such as the decree in 1854 of the Immaculate Conception, for good measure confirmed by the ridiculous dogma of the Infallibility of the Pope in 1870.The confusion was further increased when various church fathers changed, added and deleted fragments of the Bible at their convenience and also because several mistakes were made by scribes during translating and copying. Some on purpose.

There are also stories that both Jesus and Mary Magdalene had married before. Jesus to a young woman who died in childbirth. Mary Magdalene was said to be married first to John the Baptist and maybe even had a child of him. Later she was said to be married to Judas. Stories that are impossible to check, but that came to us by various channeled sources.

In the church of St. Martin in Limoux a wonderful stained glass window can be seen, showing Jesus and Mary Magdalene sitting at equal night. Some even whisper that they are holding hands behind the bar. The "official" version of the Church is however that the woman is not Mary Magdalene but Mother Mary. Ascended to Heaven and looking down together with Jesus, at the world, but I do not know. She seems a bit young to be his mother and they seem to be secretly in love.

Jesus and Mary in church St. Martin, Limoux

THE CRUCIFIXION

There are many stories about the crucifixion of Jesus. Some, including the Bible, say he died at the cross and was resurrected after three days. Where Mary Magdalene met him at the open cave and first took him for the gardener. Jesus is said to have spoken the famous words to her: "Noli me Tangere", meaning: "do not touch me". A statement that was for

ages attributed, by the Church, to the fact that Jesus was still in some kind of ethereal state. A scene that lead to hundreds of beautiful paintings. Later however it appeared that an error had been made in translating the original sentence. The correct translation was: "Don't cling to me." Which offers a totally different view of the situation.

Noli me tangere, St Maximin

According to Laurence Gardner the crucifixion took place on Friday 30th March in the year 33 AD. The hands were tied to a horizontal beam. Sometimes a nail was put through the hand. The feet rested on a small support on the vertical beam. Sometimes a nail was put through the feet. There are still discussions going on about the attachment of the feet to the cross. Would that be with ropes, with one nail or two nails?

One nail St. Maximin   *Two nails Douvre la Delivrance*

In most cases people died after two or three days. Jesus however seemed to have expired after only a few hours. To check if he was really dead the centurion Petronius stabbed him with his lance in the side, the famous lance or the Longinus. The fact that blood was coming out of the wound was taken as a sign of his death.

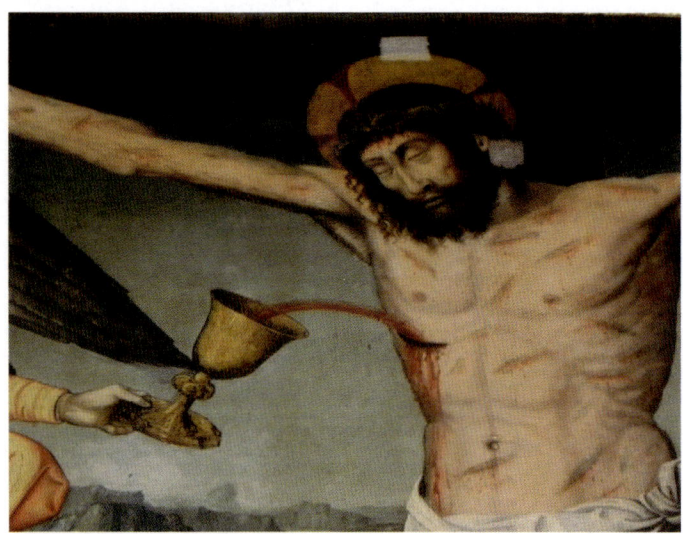
Basilica of St. Maximin

In reality it was a sign that he was still alive, for dead people do not bleed. His apparent death may have been caused by holding a sponge with a mixture of vinegar and snake poison under his face, or he might have been so well versed in controlling his bodily functions, that he could have faked his apparent death. Anyway Jacob, also named Joseph of Arimathea, his younger brother, got permission from Pontius Pilate, who was well known to Joseph and who might even have been an accomplice, to take the body off the cross before dark, before the beginning of the Sabbath.

Joseph, helped by Simon and Nicodemus, wrapped the body in a linen cloth and laid it to rest in the tomb. A huge stone was put in place to close off the tomb and two guards were placed in front of the cave. Here the stories diverge again. Some say that Jesus was still alive when he was laid in the tomb. A plausible story, confirmed by several paintings where Mary Magdalene is holding a wooden cross in her hand with leaves on the stem, as here in Rennes-le-Château. Clearly implying that this was living wood and thus that Jesus was alive.

There is also the 14th Station of the Cross in the same church dedicated to Mary Magdalene in Rennes-le-Château. Jesus is laid down in the cave, while it is dark. A full moon is clearly visible in the night sky. However, it is strictly forbidden by Jewish law to handle a corpse at nighttime, on the Sabbath and most certainly on the night before Passover. So this station also tells us that Jesus must have been alive at that moment.

Then it is said that there was another, secret entrance to the cave. Simon Zelotes was already there to receive Jesus and treat him with myrrh and Aloe. Whatever the truth, there are many stories stating that Jesus did not die on the cross. Several books have been written on this topic, such as *"Jesus after the Crucifixion, from Jerusalem to Rennes-le-Château"* by Graham Simmans. And the Islamic world never believed that Jesus, who is also one of their prophets, died on the cross.

14th Station of the Cross

Living wood, Rennes-le-Chateau

Jesus in Cave of Mary Magdalene - "Hermitage of St. Antoine", Gorges de Galamus

HER FLIGHT TO FRANCE

There are many ways leading to France. Assuming of course that Mary Magdalene went to France and did not go with John the beloved disciple to Ephesus or with Joseph of Arimathea to England. Mary Magdalene fled the country immediately after the crucifixion in 33 AD. Her flight could also have been a banishment from Palestine. Or a flight to safety, where Pontius Pilate and his wife Claudia Procula might have been involved. Mary Magdalene could have left from Palestine, Lebanon or from Egypt. With one or three boats. With boats equipped with sails, oars, a pilot and rudder or in a boat with nothing at all. Not even food. But with the help of our Lord who, according to the legend, send them an angel, a good eastern wind and sufficient food.

Beziers

But now people are starting to ask questions. Of course they do. Questions as to why wasn't it mentioned in the Bible that she was married? Or that she had children? Well first of all because the present day Bible is a heavily "concocted document", put together more than 300 years after the crucifixion, when circumstances were totally different. At the end of the 4th century Christianity changed shape, drastically. In the New Testament only 4 of the more than 60 available gospels were selected.

Christianity as laid down in the "new" bible became a state religion. Primarily meant to support the power of the emperors of Rome and later the power, the religious and secular power of the popes. In the new concocted Bible various aspects of other popular, contemporary religions were incorporated. Like Christmas and Easter. And even the 4 chosen gospels were tampered with. And these gospels contradict each other on major points. So the bible should not be taken as an accurate historical document. Nor as the word of God, burnt directly on the pages of this "Holy Book".

Apart from that, it was quite normal to be married in the 1st century AD. And highly unusual not to be married, especially for a descendant of the royal lineage of David and being rabbi on top of that.

Even more illuminating is the fact that the Bible itself explicitly mentions the marriage, twice even, but in veiled terms. So as not to arouse the suspicion of the Romans. For the Jews had much to fear from their Lords. Especially Jews that were named, or called themselves, the Messiah. And there were several self-proclaimed Messiahs at that time.

Mary Magdalene not only had to fear for her own life, but also for the life of her unborn baby. Tamar, also named Sarah. A title, meaning princess. She fled Palestine in 33 AD, some say 44 AD, but that is a mistake. Going directly to France or first to Egypt. Some say that she was recognized by a hostile Roman centurion in Alexandria and had to flee immediately. Having no time to stock the boat with food, rudder, sails and oars. The most likely scenario however is that she fled the Holy Land shortly after the crucifixion.

St. Maximim la Ste. Baume

There is an uneasy silence about the flight of Mary Magdalene to France. First it was vehemently denied, by the Church, that Mary Magdalene had "überhaupt" gone to France. In spite of the fact that in many churches paintings and stained glass windows can be seen, showing Mary Magdalene fleeing by boat. See [chapter 17](). The Church is not clear on this point. Some say that she indeed fled the first Holy Land for the second Holy Land. Others say that she stayed in Palestine. Where she could have been buried in the tomb of Talpiot, south of Jerusalem, discovered in 1980. A family tomb supposedly containing the bones of Jesus, Joseph, Maria, Mariamme (Mary Magdalene), Mattheus and Judas, son of Jesus. As far as I know it has not yet been scientifically proven or disproven that these bones really belong to Jesus and his family. And the Church, of course, is not too keen to speed up the research. They would not welcome evidence that Jesus was a mortal man, and not the Son of God. That would cause even more confusion in a Church already so disturbed.

The Church might also say that she fled to Ephesus in Turkey or to Alexandria in Egypt. Nothing can be proved right now, not with all relevant documents missing. Burned first by the Romans in 70 AD and later by the Church in the 5th and 6th century. However the most likely scenario is still that she fled to France. A scenario supported by various, ancient sources and several reliable records. As well as by old folktales and by the many pictures in churches and basilica's. Besides, it might not have been a flight, but banishment. Other

Jewish princesses had been banished to France before. Most of them to the area around Narbonne, or around Vienne, near Lyon.

Still, several things are not clear. It is not clear when she left. Was it in 33 AD immediately after the crucifixion or a little later, waiting for Jesus to recover sufficiently to travel with her. And from where? From Syria, Palestine or Egypt? It is not clear whether she left with one boat or with three and who accompanied her on her flight. Most startling of all is the fact that she supposedly sailed in a boat without sails, oars, rudder or food. Finally there is the possibility that the story of her flight to France was later, first in the 8th and 9th century and again in the 11th and 12th centuries, "adopted" by religious centers and communities along the Mediterranean, eager to establish the status of pilgrim site.

But there is more. Something different, something strange. For nowhere it is mentioned what happened to Jesus after the crucifixion. There is an uncanny silence on that topic. A bit "unheimisch" as they would say in Germany. The Church of course states that he died at the cross and was resurrected after three days. And then after 40 days ascended bodily to Heaven. But that story was, as so many other stories, slotted in later. Others say that he died at the cross and was buried somewhere in Jerusalem. Others again say that he survived the crucifixion. But was severely wounded after that ordeal and needed time to recuperate. Some say he went to the desert for 40 days to get his strength back. Others say he died shortly after the crucifixion. And some even say that Mary Magdalene took his body or his skull with her to France, as can be seen in this painting in the cave of Mary Magdalene in La Ste. Baume.

Mary Magdalene in La Ste. Baume

In the Gospel of Thomas, one of the Nag Hammadi parchments, it is stated that Jesus told his disciples, before he was crucified, to go to James, the leader of the Church of Jerusalem, in all matters of faith. James was his younger brother. See the book *"James the brother of Jesus"* written by the famous archeologist Robert Eisenmann. James was the same person as Joseph of Arimathea, the one who succeeded him. This remark could be an indication that Jesus either did not expect to survive the crucifixion, or that he did not expect to stay in the Holy Land after the crucifixion.

The most logical thing is that he fled the country, together with his pregnant wife Mary Magdalene. After all they were married, they loved each other and they needed each other, now more than ever. Besides Mary Magdalene was an excellent healer. And they were going to have two more children, Jesus II and Josephus (see chapter 10). Nobody seemed to have reached this conclusion. Why not? Why was it deemed necessary by the Church not only to blacken Mary Magdalene, but also to "separate" Jesus and Mary Magdalene? Or did Jesus really die? Or did he indeed bodily ascend to heaven 40 days after the crucifixion?

Only one writer, as far as I know, stated that Jesus and Mary Magdalene left the Holy Land together and went either to the estate of Claudia Procula, the wife of Pontius Pilate in France, or to other existing Jewish settlements in the Languedoc, more specifically in Rennes-les-Bains and in Alet-les-Bains. That writer is Val Wineyard with her books *"Mary, Jesus, and the Charismatic Priest"*, sub-titled *"Faith, Legend and Logic in Languedoc"* and her second book *"Looking for Mary M"*.

Several books have been written about Mary Magdalene's flight. Her epic voyage has been portrayed in many paintings, stained glass windows and panels like here in Aigues Mortes and in the church in Troyes, dedicated to Mary Magdalene.

Aigues Mortes

Martyrdom of Marie Magdalene, Troyes

We don't know where she landed. It could have been Marseille, an old Greek colony established in the 6th century BC. Or Saint Ferreol near what is now called Les-Saintes-Maries-de-la-Mer in the Camarque, at the mouth of the Rhone River. Or on the peninsula called Maguelone south of Montpellier. But it could also have been near Narbonne, founded by the Romans around 118 BC.

Les-Saintes-Maries-de-la-Mer

Or at the Roman Port Mahon near Sigean, between Narbonne and Perpignan. Or at Fitou, halfway between Narbonne and Perpignan. She could have landed here, at this place, for 2000 years ago there was still open water.

Fitou

Or at Sainte Marie la Mer, a small coastal village just north of Perpignan. All these places carry the memory of Mary Magdalene. Either in folktales, in paintings and statues in their churches, or in the names of hills, rivers, caves, isles and cities nearby.

Sainte Marie la Mer

Val Wineyard thinks that Jesus and Mary Magdalene landed somewhere near present day Fitou. From there Val has traced their steps all the way through the barren, desolate area near the coast to the lovely village of Rennes-les-Bains, famous for its hot springs and the mines of gold and silver. Others think that she went to the valley west of the magic mountain Pech Bugarach. See the book *"Anna, The Voice of the Magdalenes"* by Claire Heartsong. And others again think that she joined an Essene community, living on the side of the big mountain north-east of present day Couiza, called Le Camp Grand, where once over 200 small stone

Bugarach Mountain

huts, called "capitelles", stood. Or that she went to Rennes-le-Château. The route that she could have traveled is indicated on the map. Many castles, caves and churches now lie on this route.

The route of Mary Magdalene

The group that came with her to France consisted of Simon Zelotes, the leader of the group, also known as Lazarus the Great (Maximinus), Jesus' sisters Sarah-Salome, also called Maria Salome, and Maria Jacoba Cleopas and Helena-Salome the wife of Simon-Lazarus. Others say that Maria Jacoba was the mother of James and the sister of the Virgin Mary. And Maria Salome was the mother of the apostles James (known from Santiago de Compostella) and John. They are buried in the crypt of the church of Les-Stes-Maries-de-la-Mer. Also on board was Sarah-Salome, a Nazarene priestess, dressed in black. Some think that she was the maidservant of the three Maries and others think that she was the daughter of Jesus and Mary Magdalene. Or even Sara the Kali, chief of her

Sarah

tribe on the banks of the river Rhone. She now is the patron saint of the gypsies and each year her feast day is celebrated on May 24th. It is a great event, witnessed by many tourists, as her statue is carried by men on white horses from the blue waters of the Mediterranean to the sandy shore of Les-Stes-Maries-de-la-Mer and then to her place in the crypt.

The next day, May 25th, is the feast day of Saint Marie Jacobe and the third Sunday of October is Saint Marie Salome's day.

It is not clear which persons actually were in the one boat or in the three boats. Martha and Lazarus, the brother and sister of Mary Magdalene were probably also on board, as well as Martha's maid Marcella (or Martilla), and possibly also the apostle Philip.

The group soon scattered. Martha and Marcella went to Tarasçon Sur Rhône, were Martha defeated a fierce dragon with the help of a wooden cross. A bit strange this use of the cross. For the cross was only later, in the 8th century AD, introduced as the official symbol of the Christian church. But there are more examples of using the cross before its time. For example by Emperor Constantine in the early 4th century and by King Clovis in the late 6th century AD.

Ste Marie Jacoba

The church dedicated to Saint Martha in Tarasçon has some beautiful paintings of her and the dragon and of her and her sister Mary Magdalene. Maximin and Cedonius (Sidonius or Sidoine) went to Aix-en-Provence, Trophimus became the patron saint of Arles and Lazarus and Mary Magdalene went to Marseille.

Ste. Martha in Tarasçon

They can be seen in the crypt of the St. Victor church in Marseille. Maria Jacoba and Maria Salome with their maid Sarah stayed in Les-Stes-Maries-de-la-Mer, where they were so kindly received by the small fishing community living around the sweet water well near the beach. There are many more stories about Mary Magdalene. Stories coming from the East. From the Coptic Church and the Greek and Russian Orthodox Churches. The traditions of East and West started to diverge in the sixth century AD. When Christianity in the West was molded into a State religion and when Pope Gregory the Great held his infamous speech, linking Mary Magdalene to the seven deadly sins. Later in 1054 a formal schism occurred. And in 1204 Constantinople was plundered by the Crusaders. For the East European churches Mary Magdalene is also a saint, with her feast day 22nd of July. Although the dates of June 30th and August 4th are also important. In the eastern traditions Mary Magdalene is viewed as a special woman. Exactly like the woman described in the Apocrypha. And the oriental church fathers did not seem to be as scared of women as their western colleagues. In the East she is called the "Carrier of Myrrh." And she is also known as the 'Apostle of the Apostles' or the Isapostola.

St. Victor church, Marseille

Isapostola

Notre Dame de la Daurade, Toulouse

Another story, also coming from the East, describes how Mary Magdalene came to Rome and paid a visit to the emperor Tiberius. Some say to plead for the life of her beloved Jesus, others say to try and convert the emperor to Christianity. While attending a dinner party given by the emperor, she is said to have taken an egg in her hand, shouting "Christ has risen". Tiberius burst out laughing saying that a man could just as easily rise as the egg would color red. Upon which the egg turned red.

Many people still doubt if Mary Magdalene really went to France. But that can no longer be doubted, even though I realize that it is not easy to change one's beliefs. Her voyage from the first Holy Land, Palestine, to the second Holy Land, France, has been described in several authoritative documents and painted in many beautiful tableaux. See the book: *"The life of Mary Magdalen"*, written by the archbishop of Mainz, Rabanus Maurus (776-856), who gave a wonderful description of this voyage. And in the *"Legenda Aurea"*, written between 1260-1264, describing the life's of all saints, Jacobus de Voragine gives in his chapter about Mary Magdalene a vivid description of this voyage. And let us not forget Jean Cassianus, the Christian monk who served in the oldest church of Marseille, the basilica of St Victor. He traveled in the 5th century AD from Marseille to St-Maximin-la-Ste-Baume to the place where St. Maximin had buried Mary Magdalene and built a little chapel over her tomb. The chapel where later the famous basilica, dedicated to Mary Magdalene would be built. And remember the Merovingian King Clovis who, after being baptized in Reims in 496, visited the chapel where Mary Magdalene was said to be buried in 500 AD.

Mary Magdalene with the egg

WHERE DID SHE PREACH

Just as we don't know where she, or they, came on land, we also don't know where she preached. We don't even know if she preached. But she was the Apostle of the Apostles, so she must have preached. Besides she was a very determined and very convincing lady and she carried a wonderful message. In my view she preached in the whole of the South of France, in particular in the regions now called the Provence and the Languedoc. People can still feel her energy here. And almost "taste" her wonderful message, the good news that she gave to the people and to the land. It sank into the hearts of the people and was anchored in the rocks and the soil of this beautiful land. There are however, as usual, different views about where she stayed and where she preached.

Let us start with Marseille. Marseille was a big port at the time of Jesus. Founded around 600 BC by the Greeks who named it Massalia. The city was dedicated to the Goddess Artemis. The story goes that when the ship with Mary Magdalene came to Marseille she was at first not admitted by the rulers of the city. But after appearing in their dreams for three consecutive nights and threatening them with the wrath of God if they did not offer hospitality, she was admitted. In Marseille she preached against idolatry. There is a beautiful painting of her in the chapel of the Hostellerie la Sainte Baume at the foot of the Baume Mountain range. Mary Magdalene preaching in the harbor of Marseille. Her brother Lazarus was later installed as bishop in Marseille. Mary Magdalene is also said to have preached in nearby Aix-en-Provence, where Maximinus was later installed as bishop or church Father because they did not have bishops at that time.

Preaching in Marseille

Where she went after Marseille and Aix-en-Provence, we don't know. Some say that she lived in solitude for 30 years in the cave of Mary Magdalene, high up in the Baume mountain range, northeast of Marseille. But that is hard to believe. She, the Apostle of the Apostles, was not the type to live in solitude in a cave. Most likely this story got mixed up with Mary the Egyptian, who indeed lived in a cave. Besides where did her two other children, Jesus II and Josephus, come from and where did all the stories of her preaching in the rest of Provence and in the Languedoc come from? The cave is a sacred place, with the façade of a church built over the entrance. The "church" is run by Dominican monks. Every year thousands of pilgrims visit

43

the place, climbing the "Chemin des Roys", the path of the kings, starting at the famous place of the three oaks. It is a beautiful area and a wonderful pilgrim site. The cave halfway up the mountain range offers a magnificent view over the hills to the north.

Front of the cave of Mary Magdalene

View from the Cave

It is not certain that Mary Magdalene went to Marseille, St-Maximin-la-Ste-Baume, Aix-en-Provence or the cave of Ste. Baume. It is quite possible that Mary Magdalene, possibly accompanied by Joseph of Arimathea, went to what is now called the "Pays Cathare". The Cathar country, (see chapter 13). Covering roughly the departments Pyrenees Oriental, Aude, Ariège and the Taur. Possibly together with Jesus.

Why the Pays Cathare? Well, there are some good reasons for going to that area. The area around Rennes-le-Château has been considered, since times immemorial, a sacred place, a holy area. A place with two sacred mountains, the Pech Bugarach, a 1230 meter high, "male" mountain, roughly shaped and the Pech Cardou, an 800-meter high "female" mountain, shaped like a pyramid. Why these mountains are called "male" and "female", I don't know. It could be their energy or maybe their shape. The two mountains have often been compared to Mount Sinai in the Sinai desert and the Temple Mount in Jerusalem.

Pech Cardou

Pech Bugarach

Rennes-le-Château was also a sacred place of the Celts. A big altar stone found in the area, and dating from around 1000 BC, emphasizes this sacred character. And the area was well known to the Jews. Many lived there and still live in this region. It is even said that the lost tribe of Benjamin took refuge in this region after they fled Palestine.

Alter Stone in Rennes-le-Château

There is another story, stating that the Jews in the 6th century BC, yes "Before Christ", built a Temple of Solomon under the Pech Cardou. To house the Arc of the Covenant, their most sacred, religious object. For at that time Jerusalem and the Arc were seriously threatened by Nebuchadnezzar, the King of Babylon. Who conquered Judea in 586 BC, destroyed the Temple of Solomon, led the Jews in captivity to Babylon and captured all the temple treasures. But the Arc of the Covenant was not on the list of stolen artifacts.

The area around Rennes-le-Château, Rennes-les-Bains and Alet-les-Bains, was well known both to the Jews and the Romans. Several high-ranking Romans possessed land and villas in the area, among them Procula, the wife of Pontius Pilate. It is a lovely area, with beautiful rivers and valleys, fertile land and hot springs. Besides, Mary Magdalene would not have been the first woman to be banished to France. In the past several Judean princesses had been exiled to France, either to the Pays Cathare or the area around Vienne and Lyon. In Rennes-le-Château stood at the time of the Romans, a temple of Isis. That could have been another reason for Mary Magdalene to come to this place. For she was said to be one of the high priestesses of Isis. In Alet-les-Bains and in Rennes-les-Bains were settlements of wealthy Romans and Jews, enjoying the hot springs and clear waters of these places. And in Rennes-les-Rains, Rennes-le-Château and Auriac valuable minerals like gold and silver were mined. Joseph of Arimathea, the younger brother of Jesus, knew the area well. He was an important dealer in minerals. An expert in mining and a well-known tradesman. Someone who had traveled widely to all the places where minerals were found. Like the Pays Cathare. He could well have taken his brother and sister in law to this place. He also travelled to England, to Cornwall and the Mendip Hills north of Glastonbury where silver, lead and tin were mined. Tin was especially valuable, since it was used, in a 10% to 90% mixture with copper, to make bronze (see chapter 9).

And of course there are the memories of the people, the common people. Memories of where she lived, where she healed the sick and where she preached. Wonderful memories. In the oldest church in Troyes, dedicated to Mary Magdalene, we find a stained glass window depicting the life of Mary Magdalene, which includes Mary Magdalene preaching. With boards explaining the scenes.

The life of Mary Magdalene in Troyes

Explaining the Scenes

Mary Magdalene is also said to have baptized people. Four places are named; the spring of the mother Goddess in Campagne-les-Bains, the Fontaines des Amours, the fountain of lovers, in the river Sals, near Rennes-les-Bains. But also the place where the River Sals meets the river Blanque, near Rennes-les-Bains. A place called "Le Benitier", the Holy Stoup. And the Ruisseau des Couleurs, the river of colors, in Rennes-le-Château.

Very special places, with a wonderful energy. Every time I visit the spring of the mother Goddess, I feel a sense of awe, of devotion and excitement. I have witnessed several

Fontaine des Amours   *Champagne-les-Bains*

ceremonies performed there. And the Fontaine des Amours is really a fountain of lovers. Or better of "Love". It is a beautiful place, the water is flowing gently. The rocks are smooth and the whole place breathes love. And joy. All these places are within a few miles of

Rennes-le-Château. We can safely assume that Mary Magdalene, preaching her wonderful message, healing the people of the land and baptizing her followers, has made a huge impression on the people of this land.

I think that Mary Magdalene lived for a while in Rennes-le-Château. There have been several people, psychic people, who showed me the place where her house once stood. On the plain just south of the hill, at the edge of the valley of the River of Colors. It is a special place.

When I go there and look at the rocks that once might have been her house, I go quiet, very quiet. And feel close to her. As if I can touch her. Then I smile and leave the place, bowing with respect to the rocks. Others say that she lived in Rennes-les-Bains. But that she often came to the Temple of Isis and the cave of Mary Magdalene in Rennes-le-Château. Even now the hill, on which the small mountain village is situated, is called the Hill of Isis. While the hill opposite Rennes-le-Château, named Le Casteillas is called the Hill of Osiris.

Rennes-le-Château

It is possible that Mary Magdalene lived in Rennes-les-Bains and that she regularly came to Rennes-le-Château. To preach, to meditate in her cave, the cave of Mary Magdalene and to heal people. For the two Rennes are only 5 kilometers apart. Some say that Jesus was with her. Folktales tell that people actually saw him. And that he lived a quiet life. Taking care of his children and teaching the children in the area. Apparently he was, after the crucifixion, not strong enough to go out and preach. And maybe he was afraid to be recognized by hostile Roman authorities. Others say that he lived elsewhere and visited her from time to time. We don't know. What we do know is that he had two more children with Mary Magdalene

Inside cave of Mary Magdalene

(see [chapter 9)](). And some say they even had five children.

When Jesus he died or where he is buried, no one knows. Assuming of course that he survived the crucifixion. He might be buried in Rennes-le- Chateau, or in the temple of Salomon under the Pech Cardou or in St. Salvayre with its special church. A little village east of Alet-les-Bains.

The Languedoc has always been a special area, an area of free thinking people, far away from Rome, yet part of the Roman Empire. Where the Visigoth capitals of Toulouse, Carcassonne and Rhedae stood in the 5th century; and where the Merovingian kings, descendants from Jesus and Mary Magdalene ruled from the 5th to the 8th century. Where the Carolingians took over in the 8th century. During his reign Charlemagne ordered a survey of his kingdom. It was carried out by his bishops. Bishop Theodulphus reported that the city of Rhedae, as Rennes-le-Château was called then, consisted of 30,000 inhabitants. And was as big as Toulouse and Narbonne. Later a Jewish Kingdom, called Septimania, was established by Charlemagne in the Languedoc area. Then the land was ruled again by a Jewish king, a true descendent of Jesus and Mary Magdalene. A King of Davidic origin, recognized as such, on special "request" of Charlemagne, by both the Pope and the sultan of Baghdad. It was, until the 11th century, a very prosperous area where Jews, Muslims and Christians lived peacefully together. Where women had almost equal rights with men. In my view a necessary condition for a healthy and prosperous society. It was an area that knew religious freedom. A place where the troubadours sang of courtly love. Here was a Renaissance "avant la lettre". The Languedoc area flourished.

Church of St Salvayre

But alas, it could not last. During the past centuries the Church of Rome had become so decadent, so materialistic and so power hungry that they were fast losing their credibility and their followers. It was a time where bishops and priests, not to mention cardinals and popes, did about everything the Church itself had forbidden. The people of the Languedoc lost faith in the Church of Rome. They turned their back on the Church of Rome and turned to the "old" religion, the old values, the teachings of Jesus and Mary Magdalene. To their wonderful message. A message that had always been carefully guarded by the people of the land. That is how, in my opinion, the Cathars "resurfaced". Rising up from the ground dirtied by Rome. Here the seeds sown by Jesus and Mary Magdalene took fruit again. Their teachings took hold. Their message surfaced again and spread quickly.

LA SAINTE BAUME

It is said that after preaching in Marseilles, Aix-en-Provence and maybe Arles, Mary Magdalene went to a cave in the Massif-de-la-Sainte-Baume, called "Chaine de la Sainte Baume", a huge rock formation just north-east of Marseille. She supposedly lived there for 30 years. The cave is now called "the Cave of Mary Magdalene", but centuries before Mary came to that cave, it was already a sacred place. A place that was later, as happened with so many sacred places, Christianized by the Church. It is doubtful whether Mary Magdalene actually lived there, for 30 years, in complete solitude. I think the story was concocted by the Church to mask the fact that, during those years, she preached in the south of France, in the Provence and the Languedoc. It is also possible that the story got mixed up with the story of St. Mary the Egyptian, who really lived in a cave, after a sinful life.

Massif-de-la-Sainte-Baume

At the foot of this massive mountain range, in a place called Plan-d'Aups-Ste-Baume, is a hotel, run by nuns of the Dominican Order. It is called the Hotellerie de la Sainte Baume. With simple, clean rooms and a beautiful chapel, called "La Chapelle de Marie Madeleine". In the chapel are four magnificent frescos of Mary Magdalene. Among them one where she is standing in front of the cave, preaching to the fishermen of Marseille and one being lifted up to heaven.

There are also several statues of Mary Magdalene. The nuns are gentle, but strict. They stick to the rules and you too are expected to stick to the rules, their rules. No filming or photographing in the chapel during services. The meals are served on time and you eat what they serve you. But, fortunately, there is also wine on the table. After all we are in France. From the Hotellerie it is a short walk to the "Three

Hotellerie de la Sainte Baume

Oaks", the starting point for the "Chemin des Roys". Very ancient trees. Unfortunately only one of them survived to this day.

Many kings visited the cave. Like Saint Louis, Rene d'Anjou, Philip VI, John the Good, Charles VI and VII, Louis XI, Francois I, Charles IX, Henry II with Catherine the Medici, Louis XIII and Louis XIV. The climb to the cave takes about 20-30 minutes, the last part climbing the stairs. The cave is guarded by Dominican monks. It is a beautiful place with a magnificent view.

"Three" oaks

Statue of Mary Magdalene

Dominican Monk

Stairs to the cave

Before you reach the cave, you will see on your left hand side a vivid and lifelike scene of the crucifixion. In the church are many statues, stained glass windows and relics of Mary Magdalene. Outside, on the square in front of the church building, you will find a wonderful statue of the Pieta. Mother Mary and Mary Magdalene mourning the death Jesus. With Mary Magdalene kneeling by the side of Jesus

In the rest room another lovely picture of Mary Magdalene can be seen. All very moving. In 2009 there was an exposition celebrating the 150th anniversary of the establishment of the Dominicans at la-Sainte-Baume.

View from cave

Crucifixion next to cave

Pieta in front of cave

There is a strange story with respect to the safeguarding of her relics during the time when the Saracens, the Spanish called them the Moors, conquered the South of France. A story told by the learned Dominican friar Père Jean-Baptiste-Henri Dominique Lacordaire (1802-1861). In the 8th century AD the Saracens belonging to the caliphate of Baghdad had their French capital in Narbonne and a strong outpost in Nimes. So they were pretty close to the chapel in Baume. As a precaution the Cassianite monks removed the relics of Mary Magdalene from her alabaster tomb and put them in the tomb of St. Sidoine. Together with a written explanation of what they had done. We now know that Charles Martel stopped the Saracens in 732 at Poitiers. After which they were slowly but steadily pushed back over the Pyrenees. Narbonne was recaptured in 759 by Pepin the Short, with the help of the Jewish community of that city.

In the 11th century it became known that the tomb of Mary Magdalene at Ste. Baume was empty. It was rumored that Gerard de Roussillon, former governor of the Provence, had transferred the bones to the abbey in Vezelay. The bishop of Autun and Vezelay, worried that Vezelay would become a tourist attraction, denied the existence of these relics and asked the Pope to negate the story. A rather unusual step for a bishop, I would think. Most of them would welcome such valuable relics.

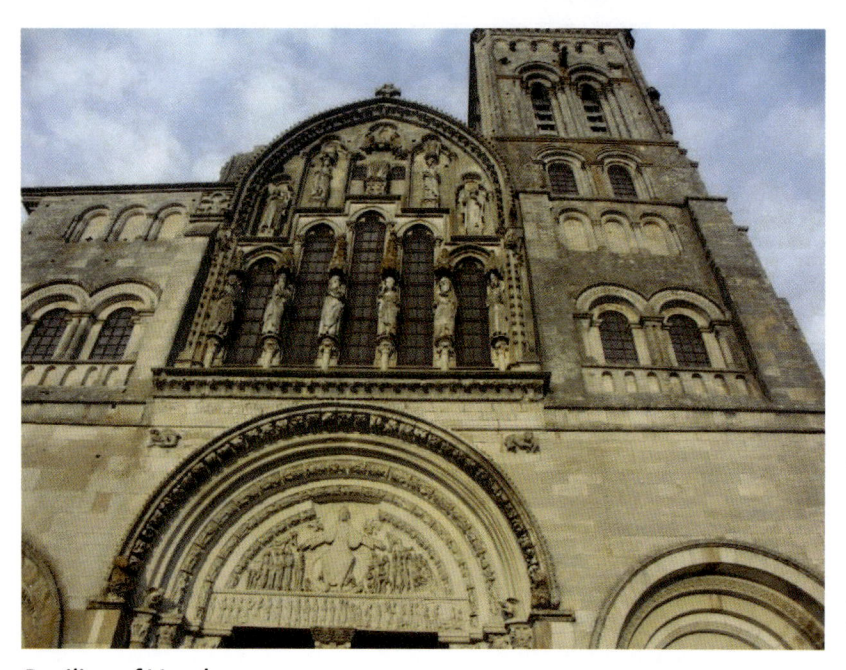

Basilica of Vezelay

But surprise, surprise, Pope Paschalis II confirmed the existence of the relics in Vezelay. He was apparently quite happy with this new pilgrim site. Then, from 1096, onwards the old abbey was converted into a beautiful basilica dedicated to Mary Magdalene. It became a famous pilgrim site. In 1147 King Louis VII, Queen Eleanor and Bernardus of Clairvaux summoned their followers to Vezelay where they called for a second crusade to the Holy land. Bernardus, the powerful abbot of Clairvaux, had arranged in 1128 that all Templars swore an oath of loyalty to the house of Bethany, (see chapter 14), thus linking Mary Magdalene to the Knights Templar and the crusades. In 1189 King Philip Auguste and Richard Lionheart called for a third crusade, also in Vezelay.

In 1279 King Louis IX started wondering what proof there was for the existence of the relics of Mary Magdalene in Vezelay. Could it all have been a hoax? So he went to Baume, talked to the monks and was told that the story of the bones being transferred to Vezelay was indeed not true. It was just a rumor. He was furious. Later that year, on December 18th 1279 AD, King Louis, accompanied by King Charles of Naples, by the bishops of Aix and Arles and by many other officials broke the seals on the sarcophagus of Sidonius. There they found a parchment written by the Cassianite Monks, stating that in 710 AD, as a precaution, they had transferred the bones of Mary Magdalene to the tomb of Sidonius. The fraud was made public and from 1280 onwards many dignitaries visited the "newly discovered" tomb of Mary Magdalene.

Skull of Mary Magdalene

Her skull was set in gold and precious stones, coming from the crown provided by King Charles I of Anjou. It took all of 5 years before Pope Bonifacius VIII finally stated in a bull that these were the true relics of Mary Magdalene. The cloister of Saint-Maximin was then transferred to the care of the Dominican Order. Mary Magdalene became their patron saint. Funds were provided for building a large basilica dedicated to Mary Magdalene on the site of the old chapel of the Cassianites.

See further chapter 8.

It took almost 200 years to build the basilica. In spite of the support of the Dominicans and of King René d'Anjou (1408-1480), one of the most fervent admirers of Mary Magdalene. Together with his wife Jehanne de Laval he organized Magdalene pilgrimages, built a church for Martha in Tarasçon sur Rhone, organized the popular Bethany festivals and was president of the Les Saintes Maries festivals. After that many kings made a pilgrimage to La Sainte Baume. Among them king Louis XI (1461-1483), who called Mary Magdalene "The Daughter of France" and Louis XIV together with his mother Anne of Austria.

During the construction of the basilica no less than 5 kings, from all over Europe, visited this site on one single day. And no less than 8 popes visited her shrine in one century. Isn't it amazing that so many dignitaries, including popes, cardinals, bishops, abbots and kings, visited her tomb? The tomb of Mary Magdalene, the woman who was vilified by the Church. The woman who was "officially" labeled a repentant sinner (see chapter 11). But then it always amazed me that truly religious people can be such true hypocrites, capable of doing truly awful things, without showing any true sign of remorse.

During the fierce religious wars with the Protestants, the Huguenots, (1562-1598) many beautiful monuments and shrines were destroyed. During the French revolution (1789-1799) many more religious sites were plundered. What a senseless destruction! And what awful brutalities were committed in the name of Christ. This kind of behavior was most likely caused by the power hungry Church of Rome. And later, at the time of the French Revolution by the combined power of the Church and the French nobility. La Sainte-Baume too suffered under this onslaught. Fortunately many relics were saved. In 1822, when people had come to their senses again, the basilica was restored and most relics were returned to their rightful place.

La Madeleine, Paris

Mary Magdalene was reinstated as the mother of France. Maybe she was secretly compared to Marianne, the symbol of the French revolution. She even looked like Mary Magdalene. Anyway in 1842 an imposing new church was dedicated to Mary Magdalene. It was the Madeleine, in Paris, a building originally meant as a temple for the soldiers of Napoleon.

Now converted to a church. This church reflects in a wonderful way the love and passion of the French for Mary Magdalene, Queen of France.

Inside la Madeleine

RENNES-LE-CHÂTEAU

Rennes-le-Château has been mentioned before. It is a sacred place. A place everyone knew about, except the people who lived there. Many stories about Rennes-le-Château have already been told in chapter 5. Explaining why Mary Magdalene came to this area. Stories about a temple of Lemuria, about an outpost of Atlantis, about the two sacred mountains, the Pech Bugarach and the Pech Cardou. Stories about the new Temple of Salomon, built under the Pech Cardou. Possibly housing the Arc of the Covenant, the tombs of Jesus and Mary Magdalene and maybe the Menorah. It is also said that Jesus and Mary Magdalene were two of the 12 guardians of this temple. Stories about the temple of Isis on the hill where Rennes-le-Château is situated. No wonder that Rennes-le-Château is sometimes called the "New Jerusalem". And stories about Claudia Procula having a house in Rennes-les-Bains.

Rennes-le-Château

In the area around Rennes-le-Château many places refer to Mary Magdalene and Jesus. Like the cave of Mary Magdalene directly opposite Rennes-le-Château. Many places contain the name "Madeleine", such as the "Source Madeleine", the spring of Mary Magdalene. Then there are places called L'Homme Mort, the dead man, or La Valdieu, the vessel of God. Several churches in this area are dedicated to Mary Magdalene or contain special chapels ornamented with beautiful pictures, statues and stained glass windows of Mary Magdalene. A few churches in the area also house statues of the "Black Virgin". See chapter 16.

Cave of Mary Magdalene Rennes-le-Château

57

In my view Mary Magdalene, first or finally, came to this area after fleeing Palestine or Egypt. She could have taken several routes. Maybe she went first to Les-Stes-Maries-de-la-Mer or Marseille and from there to Aix-en-Provence and Arles. It is possible. She could have traveled along the coast from Marseille to Narbonne. There are many places along this route where she is still remembered and honored, like Aigues Mortes, Maguelone, Sète and Agde. She could also have taken a more inland route, passing places like Tarasçon-sur-Rhone where Martha stayed, Beaucaire which still houses a chapel dedicated to her, St Gilles and then on to Beziers, with a church dedicated to Mary Magdalene and finally to Narbonne, with the cathedral of St-Just and St-Pasteur.

Maguelone

Narbonne

Notre Dame du Cros

Or further north via St Pons de Thomières, Minerve, Caunes Minervois with the lovely church of Notre Dame du Cros, to Carcassonne.

But I am convinced that she finally came to the area of Rennes-le-Château, Rennes-les-Bains, Alet-les-Bains and Bugarach.

Cave of Perillos

She could also have landed directly in Narbonne, or in some remote spot near Fitou or in a place called Sainte-Marie-la-Mer, east of Perpignan and made her way from there to Rennes-le-Château, using secondary roads, or tracks. Val Wineyard has carefully traced the steps of Jesus and Mary Magdalene from Fitou to Rennes-les-Bains. Passing places like Opoul-Perillos with its famous cave, Vingrau, Tuchan, Padern, Cucugnan with the statue of "Maria Enceinte", the pregnant Mary, the Cathar castles of Queribus and Peyrepertuse, Soulatge, Cubières with its chapel of Mary Magdalene, Bugarach with its church with strange stained glass windows and finally Rennes-les-Bains. Is not it striking to see how many sacred places now line the route that she probably took?

Cucugnan

Bugarach

The churches and Cathar castles did of course not exist at that time, but were built later. It is a track that runs almost parallel to the well-known "Sentier Cathare", the footpath of the Cathars. The sentier, running from Port-la-Nouvelle on the Mediterranean coast to Foix, halfway the Pyrenees.

Mary Magdalene probably lived in a house on the plateau south of the village. Three psychics showed me the place where she lived. They were all different places, okay, but no more than a hundred meters apart. And she could have moved from one place to another. I have investigated all these sites and I don't know. All three places hold a special energy, but the most "tantalizing" energy came from the place with the stones.

The house of Mary Magdalene? Rennes-le-Château

That place was also closest to the path from the plateau to the Cave of Mary Magdalene. She often went to the cave across the Ruisseau de Couleurs, the River of Colours. To pray, to meditate and to make contact, deep inside the cave, with Mother Earth.

In that cave she received many visitors, gave them advice, preached and cured people, mostly women who were in labor or had been hurt, abused or raped. I participated in several channeling sessions in that cave, channeling

Cave of Mary Magdalene, Rennes-le-Château

Mary Magdalene. They were beautiful and often very moving stories. I even have a video recording of a channeled session that lasted over 20 minutes. The tears flowed down my cheek when I listened to her "voice.", for I was there too, long ago. As her guard, her guide and her messenger boy. She was happy in that cave and she did a lot of good work. The people came from far to visit her. They loved her as I did. And still do.

Next to the Cave of Mary Magdalene is another cave, only recently explored. The cave is called her birthing cave. It looks like a vagina. Inside the cave it looks and feels like a womb. I have witnessed several people reliving their birthing process in that cave. Very emotional. Some crying out in pain, some laughing and happy, but most of them weeping softly. And quite recently a third cave was discovered, at the same location. A cave with a high energy. I named this cave "the cave of Jesus". So now there are three caves at this sacred location, like a Holy Trinity.

Birthing cave

There is a curious, channeled story that after many years Mary Magdalene left Rennes-le-Château. She is said to have traveled with a small group of followers to Avalon in England, the present day city of Glastonbury in Somerset. Passing on her way north the city of Avalon in France, near Auxerre. Her task was to activate on her way from Rennes-le-Château to Avalon, all the sacred places of Isis. However she was betrayed near Vezelay and brutally murdered. Her body was burned and her ashes were dispersed over the land. How strange that this should happen close to Vezelay. The place that was to become, nine centuries later, one of the most important pilgrim sites of France, with a huge basilica dedicated to Mary Magdalene.

Others say that she traveled with Joseph of Arimathea to England, to Glastonbury and from there to Wales. Others again say that she stayed in Rennes-le-Château, died there and was buried

Basilica of Vezelay

either in the Temple of Solomon under the Pech Cardou, or in a crypt under the present day church of Rennes-le-Château. Or in the Martyrium just south of the village or maybe in

Limoux where now stands the basilica the Notre Dame de Marceille. But there are more contenders for her tomb, or her remains, as you will see in chapter 8.

Rennes-le-Château was a big city around 800 AD when the emperor Charlemagne ordered a review of all the important possessions of his empire. Rhedae as it was called then had 30,000 inhabitants and was as big as Toulouse and Carcassonne. For a few centuries it was part of the Jewish Kingdom, Septimania, established by the emperor Charlemagne and ruled by descendents from the House of David. Then ill luck befell the city. It was caught up in a power struggle between the counts of Barcelona and the counts of Carcassonne. Both claimed possession of this area. Rhedae was twice destroyed by the troops of the count of Barcelona, once in the 11th and once in the 12th century. It was not too difficult, for Spain was close. Many people don't realize that the Roussillon, the region to the southeast of Rennes-le-Château, only ten miles away, belonged to the crown of Catalonia. That was until the treaty of 1656 when a new frontier between Spain and France was established. This frontier, which is the present day frontier, runs over highest summits of the Pyrenees.

Later, Rhedae suffered badly from the Albigensian Crusade, 1209 – 1244 AD, where more than 300,000 true believers were killed by their fellow Christians. See chapter 13. In 1232 the papal inquisition was installed by Pope Gregory IX and did its gruesome work. Thousands and thousands of innocent Christians were tortured and killed. This horrible period was followed by marauders and brigands coming from Spain/Roussillon. Next was the terrible 100-year war with England with the infamous Black Prince ravishing Aquitania and parts of the Languedoc. Then the plague, or the Black Death, struck, twice, killing about 30 % of the population. This was followed by the religious wars with the Huguenots in the 16th century and finally the French revolution at the end of the 19th century. The Pays Cathare suffered so badly from all these horrors that is has been at its last gasp during the past two centuries, with an apotheosis in the two world wars in the 20th century. All these disasters however kept the area pure, unspoiled and poor, one of the reasons why it is so beautiful now. And why the people are so nice and hospitable. Only now the area is slowly recovering.

The present day Rennes-le-Château is most famous for of its 'million dollar priest,' Berenger Saunière. He lived in this magical village from 1885 until his death in 1917. I cannot even begin to tell you all the stories, secrets, intrigues, myths, hypotheses, treasure hunts, extortions, secret societies, church pressures and even murders, related to Saunière, his predecessor Bigou and his colleagues Boudet of Rennes-les-Bains and Gelis of Coustaussa. But I can tell you that more than 600 books have been written about this place and related topics, including five of mine. Saunière spent about 30 million euro's, present price-level, on his church, his domaine with the Belvedère, the Orangerie, the Tour Magdala, the Villa Bethania, his garden, his travels and his lavish parties. He had plans for constructing a road from Couiza to the village, building a water tower and erecting a new, 60-meter high tower, next to the Tour Magdala. The present day church was originally the chapel of the Hautpoul Castle. It was dedicated to Mary Magdalene in 1059.

Tour Magdela

Berenger Saunière

The little church is famous. It is a special church. The church contains 96 anomalies of what is normal in a small catholic church in the South of France. And as you can guess, every single one of those anomalies has given rise to speculations as to where the treasure or treasures are buried and to what the awesome secret is. But up to this day we don't know, we still don't know. We don't know what the treasure is. Was it gold, or relics or "hot" documents? We don't know where the treasures were or are buried. And most of all, we don't know what his secret was.

But I am not too much interested in where the treasure is buried. Saunière will have kept

Church of Rennes-le-Château

that a secret. I am far more interested in what he did with his money. Why he traveled so extensively in search of Mary Magdalene. To, as far as we know now, Lyon and Le Pilat, Paris, Vienna and even Budapest. Or closer, to Perpignan and Perillos. And why he did meet with so many secret societies? Was he a freemason or a member of other societies which were plentiful, and very powerful, at that time? Why did he meet with members of royal families, like the Bourbons and Hapsburgs? And with very prominent, spiritual people. Why did he receive such huge gifts, often anonymous? But most of all "why Mary Magdalene?" Why is everything he did, in his church, in his visits, in his wanderings through the countryside, pointing to Mary Magdalene? What did he discover? What was his message? What is the meaning of all the anomalies in his church?

We can only guess. Is Mary Magdalene buried somewhere near Rennes-le-Château? Did Saunière know about the bloodline of Jesus and Mary Magdalene? Did he find secret documents or holy relics like the Arc of the Covenant and the Menorah? Did he know who the real father of Louis XIV was? Did he know about the Priory of Sion and the "Grand Monarch? We don't know. It is still a mystery. A mystery that attracts many people. Most certainly after the bestsellers *"The Holy Blood and the Holy Grail"* and *"The Da Vinci Code"* and maybe the DVD *"Bloodline"*. Now over 130,000 people visit this little mountain village every year. Most of them in the months of July and August.

Mary Magdalene is very much present in Rennes-le-Château and the area around that mystical village. In the church, dedicated to her. In the bookshops, carrying hundreds of books about her. In the Tour Magdala, the Villa Bethania and the garden of Saunière, which is now a restaurant where people like to meet, talk and listen to the music of visiting musicians.

The energy of Mary Magdalene can even be seen rising out of the trees at Les Labadous, my home. Like a beam of white light erupting from the earth, so I was told by some psychic friends who stayed at my place and witnessed this phenomenon from far off.

Villa Bethania, Rennes-le-Château

There is even an image of Mary Magdalene accentuated in the bark of one of the huge black poplar trees. A special tree. Many people go there. Embracing that tree and other trees along the river.

Crying, signing, laughing or meditating for hours in front of the trees. Enjoying and embracing the energy of Mary Magdalene.

Mary Magdalene outlined in rind of the tree *Embracing the tree*

Even the ORBS, those beautiful and magic flying bulbs love to be near that tree.

ORBS at Mary Magdalene Tree at Les Labadous

Let us have a look at some of the pictures, statues, stained glass windows, panels and curious texts that Saunière left to us. Especially at the Stations of the Cross. And stare in wonder at the buildings he put up on his domain. Let us then create our own myths, truths and "treasure" hunts. For the real treasure might not be gold, secret documents or a terrible secret. It could be just as well a spiritual secret. And it probably is.

Panel of Mary Magdalene below alter

Station of the Cross VIII

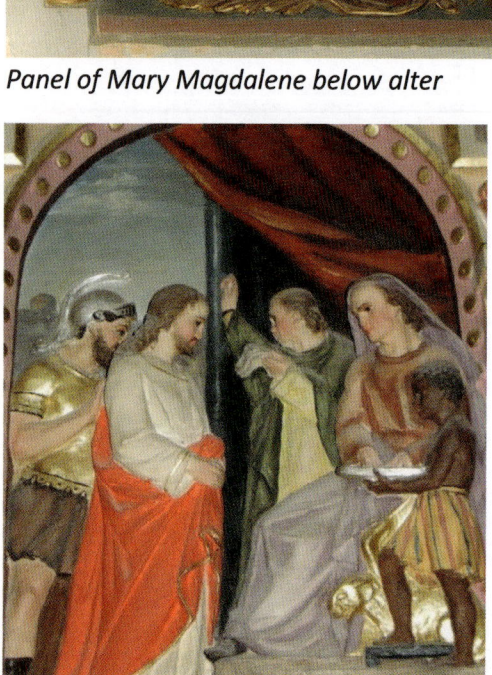

Station of the Cross I

Upper panel Jesus preaching in the hills

66

HER FINAL RESTING PLACE

Mary Magdalene is said to have died in 63 AD in the Provence. Maximin had been forewarned that her end was near and went to the cave in Ste Baume to pick her up. Or she could have gone to St-Maximin-la-Ste-Baume herself, where she was administered the last sacraments. She was buried by St. Maximin in St-Maximum-la-Ste-Baume. Others say that she was buried in Aix-en-Provence. And others again say that her last wish was to be buried in Vezelay. All places that have been battling for ages for the honor of housing her bones or part of her bones. Involving popes, kings and bishops in their fight. There is even the story that she might be buried at the ancient cemetery on the peninsula of Maguelone.

Maguelone

Now her skull and some of her bones are said to rest in the crypt of the Basilica in St-Maximin-la-Ste-Baume. And maybe some of her bones were transferred to the Cave of Ste Baume.

Crypt in basilica St. Maxmin

Cave of St. Baume

Crypt of St. Maximin

Jean Cassian, or Cassianus, who created the Cassianiter Order in 410 AD, traveled from Marseille to her final resting place in St-Maximin-la-Ste-Baume and built a chapel over the place where she was supposed to be buried. Her tomb was visited in 500 AD by the Merovingian King Clovis, who was in the process of conquering what now is called France.

It is also possible that Mary Magdalene is buried somewhere in or near Rennes-le-Château. Possibly in the temple of Solomon under the Pech Cardou. Or in a crypt deep under the present day church in Rennes-le-Château, where once the Temple of Isis stood. Or in one of the many caves under the plateau south of the village. Or in the Martyrium at the foot of Rennes-le-Château.

Pech Cardou

There are even stories that she is buried in the vaults of the Notre Dame de Marceille, just north of Limoux, 15 miles from Rennes-le-Château.

Notre Dame de Marceille

Then there is the story that Gerard de Roussillon brought the remains of Mary Magdalene from St-Maximin-la-Ste-Baume to Vezelay. To keep them out of the hands of the Saracens who, in the 8th century AD, had conquered most of the south of France.

Crypte in Vezelay

In the crypt of the basilica is still a piece of her. Another story relates how one of his successors, returning from the Holy Land after the Crusades, brought the remains of Mary Magdalene to Le Pilat, near Vienne, south of Lyon. There is also the story, mentioned in chapter 7, that Mary Magdalene with some of her followers, left Rennes-le-Château for Avalon in England. While reactivating all the sacred sites of Isis en route. And that she was betrayed near Vezelay

Her body was burned and her ashes dispersed. How strange that this should happen near Vezelay, which was later to become one of the major pilgrim sites of Mary Magdalene.

There are other stories. Of course there are. For example that she traveled with her daughter Sarah and with Joseph of Arimathea to England, to Glastonbury. And that she was buried either in Glastonbury, in "the holiest earth" of England, where now the Lady Chapel of the former Abbey stands. The place where Jesus II, the eldest son of Jesus and Mary Magdalene, together with his uncle Joseph of Arimathea, founded the first Christian church, a wattle church, in 64 AD. The church that he dedicated to his mother, Mary Magdalene. Although others say it was dedicated to Mother Mary.

There is a stone in the wall of the Lady Chapel carrying the names of Jesus and Mary.

The Abbey of Glastonbury

Jesus Maria stone

There is also the story that at the end of her life, she went to Wales, where she lived in a small cottage on the coast. And that she was taken over sea, after her death, to the sacred earth of Avalon, as shown by this picture on a shield found on Beckery Island near Glastonbury

There is even a story that she might be buried in or around the Lincoln Cathedral in England.

Mary Magdalene carried back to Avalon

And there is of course the "official" story, the story of the Roman Catholic Church. They say that she is buried in Ephesus. And that her relics were later removed and transferred, on the 4th of May, another feast day, to Constantinople by order of the 9th century emperor of the Eastern Roman empire, Leo VI. But then, she could also be buried in the family tomb of Jesus, which was discovered in 1980 in the district of Talpiot, in the south of Jerusalem.

One curious fact remains. Which is the reverence paid to Mary Magdalene throughout the ages. By everyone. Men, women, royalty, noble houses, abbots and monks, yes even by popes, cardinals, bishops and priests. Why? Why did they honor her? Why did they build basilicas to house her remains. Why did they visit her tomb or tombs. Why? In spite of the blackening of her image by the Church. In spite of the fact that she was officially labeled a repentant sinner. In spite of the fact that the Gnostic gospels were declared heretical. In spite of the persecution of the Cathars and the suppression of the Knights Templar. In spite of the domination of the Western World by men, right till the 20th century.

In spite of all that Mary was honored and revered in Europe. Why was this women honored above all others, even by the Church, with maybe one exception. Mother Mary. Why?

JOSEPH OF ARIMATHEA

Who was he? Was he a high priest of Jerusalem? A skillful craftsman? A "connoisseur" and trader in valuable minerals? An important official? A rich merchant? A good friend of Pontius Pilate? We don't know. Maybe he was all of that. What was his relation to Jesus? Were they family? Was Joseph his father, stepfather, uncle or his brother? We don't know. Not for sure. With Laurence Gardner I think that Joseph was Jesus' younger brother. Therefore I will, again, follow his views with respect to the story of Joseph of Arimathea.

Joseph is also known as Jacob the Just, or Jacobus Justus. He was born in the year 1 AD and was, after Jesus, next in line for the dynastic Davidic succession. That's why he got the title "Joseph". He also held the title "Arimathea", meaning: "Divine Highness" or "Divine Holiness". After the crucifixion Joseph took over from Jesus. When questions would arise about religious topics Jesus had often said to his disciples, before his crucifixion: "Where ever you are, go to Jacob the Just".

What happened to him after the crucifixion is not clear. There are several, different stories. Some say that Joseph was apprehended for breaking the law. Joseph and Nicodemus had been tending to Jesus when he was taken off the cross, a serious crime. For that he was jailed. Some say Jesus appeared before him in jail and gave him the cup that was used to capture his blood while hanging on the cross. A cup with magical powers. The Holy Grail. Others say it was the cup used at the last supper, also a Holy Grail. Some say that Jesus initiated him in the mysteries of the Eucharist. Some say he stayed in prison for 7 years and was kept alive by the physical and spiritual food provided by the cup. Others say that a dove brought him a host every day. Others say that he escaped from prison. We will never know. Even the most interesting, channeled books provide no conclusive answers.

Church of St. Volusien, Foix

It is generally agreed however that Joseph was convicted in 62 AD to be stoned to death for his, supposed, involvement in the murder of the high priest Ananus.

Joseph of Arimathea, Foix   *Joseph of Arimathea, Glastonbury*

His stoning was not a real execution, but banishment for life. Joseph left for England, the country where he had been before as a "decurio", a crafty metalworker and a good tradesman. England, and especially the areas of Cornwall and of the Mendip Hills north of Glastonbury, rich in minerals like lead, silver and tin. On his way to England he may have visited Mary Magdalene in France. Joseph was, and still is, very important for England and for Christianity. He was part of the Holy Family, being one of the children of Joseph and Mother Mary. He too could trace his lineage back to King David. He brought with him the original teachings of his brother Jesus and his sister in law Mary Magdalene. Teachings that blended nicely with the views of the druids, merging into a new religion. Leading eventually to a new church, the Celtic Church. He also brought with him the cup used at the last supper. And the two cruets with the blood and sweat of Jesus while he was hanging on the cross.

When he arrived in Glastonbury he planted his staff in the ground on Wearyall Hill. From this staff sprouted the famous Holy Thorn, a tree that, only in Glastonbury and its immediate surroundings, blossoms both at Christmas and at Easter. In England the royal families welcomed him. King Arvirargus who ruled over Siluria, covering most of present day Somerset, gave him 12 hides of land, roughly 1440 acres, or 580 hectares. Arvirargus was the brother of Caracatus, the Pendragon, the upper dragon, or the King of kings in England. Joseph of Arimathea married princes Enygeusa, the sister of King Arvirargus. From this marriage a second, sacred Bloodline was started in Great Britain.

Joseph visited Glastonbury on two or three occasions. The last time was in 62 AD. Some say that he arrived in Glastonbury in that year accompanied by 12 disciples and by his nephew Jesus II. In 63 AD he built the first Christian church in England, and maybe the first Christian church in the world, on the land given to him by his brother in law King Arvirargus. It was a "wattle church", made of the branches of willow trees and covered with mud. It was called the "vetusta ecclesia", the old church. In 64 AD Jesus II dedicated this church to his mother, Mary Magdalene. Others say that Joseph dedicated it to his mother, the Virgin Mary. A stone in the wall of the Lady Chapel, with the text "JESUS MARIA" still reminds us of this memorable occasion.

Jesus II arriving in Glastonbury

Joseph with his staff

This wattle church became the holiest spot in England. Revered by the hermits who lived around the church. Honored by the Irish with St. Patrick as the first abbot of what was later to become the magnificent abbey of Glastonbury, the most important abbey in England, after Westminster abbey.

Visited by thousands of pilgrims. Blessed by holy men. Respected by all Saxon kings and Norman kings right up to the disastrous Dissolution Act of 1539, the act drawn up by the frustrated King Henry VIII. Confiscating all Churches and Abbeys. Causing the abbey to become one of the most beautiful ruins in the world.

The Abbey of Glastonbury

There are several stories about Mary Magdalene in Glastonbury. She is said to have visited the place twice. Once accompanied by Joseph of Arimathea and/or by Anna, her mother in law who may have been born in Cornwall and once by her son Jesus II. Others say that she lived for several years in a cave under Chalice Hill with her daughter Sarah. She is well remembered in Glastonbury. St. Brigid, a disciple of St. Patrick, built in the 5th century AD a chapel dedicated to Mary Magdalene on the isle of Beckery. Another chapel dedicated to her was built in the 12th century as part of two almshouses. Her statue can still be seen in the Bell Tower and there is a beautiful portrait of her in the chapel. There is also a Magdalene street where once a fountain stood dedicated to Mary Magdalene.

Bell Tower on the chapel of St. Mary Magdalene

Her Portrait in the chapel

74

In Taunton, not far from Glastonbury, is a beautiful church dedicated to Mary Magdalene. With wonderful pictures, stained glass windows, statues and standards of this extraordinary

Church of Taunton

Mary Magdalene with cup

woman. More than I have seen in any other church with the exception of the churches of St-Maximin-la-Ste-Baume, the church of Stes-Maries-de-la-Mer and the church of Rennes-le-Château.

Glastonbury is a town with a strong female energy. *The energy of Mary Magdalene*. The town has two officially registered Goddess temples housing the Goddesses of Nature. There are goddesses in wall paintings. There are statues of beautiful women. And out in the street you will find many beautiful and elegant women, "live" women. Very gracious, very feminine and very powerful. It is a city of joy, festivities, ceremonies, and celebration. Think of the yearly Rock festival in May in nearby Pilton, visited by over 100.000 young people. And the carnivals in November.

Inside the Goddess Temple

It is a city of healing and contemplation. Nowhere else in the world have I seen so many healing centers, offering so many therapies. A city where sacred femininity is tangible. Where it is alive and kicking. Where the ancient Gods of Avalon, the Gods of the Tor and the sacred springs are gently merging with the Christian Gods and saints of Glastonbury. The

Gods and saints of the abbey, chapels and churches. Where new ideas and new insights appear. Where a new, Gnostic religion is born. A holy place, a city of love.

Anna the daughter of Joseph Arimathea and the princess Enygeus was married to Bran the Blessed, a nephew of the former Pendragon Cymbeline, King of the Catuvellani. They became the ancestors of several royal families in Wales, Cornwall, Scotland and England. Laurence Gardner did not only trace the bloodline of Jesus and Mary Magdalene but also the bloodline of Joseph of Arimathea and Enygeusa, with surprising results. See the book *"The Grail Enigma, the hidden descent of Jesus"*. Here I will present some of his most remarkable findings.

Joseph first came to Siluria in the South of England in 35 AD. In 37 AD he married Enygeus (Enygeusa), daughter of the King Cymbeline, the Pendragon (upper king) and sister of Caratacus and Arvirargus. The offspring of Joseph and Enygeus are also considered to be part of the Desposyni, the descendants of the Holy Family, being Father Joseph and the Virgin Mary. The Church however, according to Laurence Gardner, only regarded the offspring of Jesus and Mary Magdalene as belonging to the Desposyni.

Funny how Church logic sometimes works. For Jesus was not supposed to be married at all, let alone to have children! I will not elaborate about the offspring of Joseph of Arimathea and Enygeusa. Just read the books of Laurence Gardner. There is however one thing I would like to mention.

It is truly remarkable that where the bloodlines "met", the one from Jesus and Mary Magdalene in France and the one from Joseph and Enygeusa in Great Britain, where they intermarried, some very powerful kings and queens were born. Like King Arthur, and Clovis and Henry II, who married the equally powerful Eleanor of Aquitaine. Arthur, for example was the son of Aedàn, King of Dalriade and Pendragon and the beautiful Ygerna del Acqs (Igraine) who came from Avalon in France. Both were descendants through different lines of the Fisher kings.

Joseph of Arimathea died on 27th of July in the year 82 AD, again according to Laurence Gardner. He is probably buried somewhere in Glastonbury, either under Wearyall Hill, under Chalice Hill or in the "Holiest Earthe" next to the wattle church.

A picture of the famous Tor, with the sun setting on this imposing hill at Christmas time. And the famous Holy Thorn on Wearyall Hill.

The Tor in Glastonbury

The Holy Thorn on Wearyall Hill

THE DESPOSYNI

I am still following the story of Laurence Gardner, who did a lot of research on the genealogies of Jesus and Mary Magdalene. His findings do not always correspond with mine, but that doesn't matter. There are so many views in existence, that it won't make much difference. And his story is a consistent one. Tracing both the ancestors of Jesus and Mary Magdalene and their family members and those of Joseph of Arimathea, Jesus' younger brother and his English wife. See his book *"BLOODLINE of the HOLY GRAIL"*.

Jesus in St. Maximim

Laurence Gardner traced the bloodline of Jesus and Mary Magdalene all the way back to King David. His genealogy runs from King David (1008-1001 BC) to King Arthur (559-603 AD). In his book *"The Serpent Grail"* published in 2005, written together with Gary Osborn, he even traces the ancestry of Jesus back to the ancient Gods, to Tiamat, the Dragon queen and Aspu, Lord of the Waters. Fascinating stuff.

Recently an interesting DVD and book appeared on Jesus and Mary Magdalene. The authors claimed to have found, near Rennes-le-Château, the embalmed body of a woman from the first century AD, coming from the Middle East. Possibly Mary Magdalene. No firm authentication has been made so far. And I don't know if I can believe what the author Ben Hammott states. For both the body and the linen garments seem to be in excellent condition, which is pretty strange, to state it mildly, given the overall weather conditions in France.

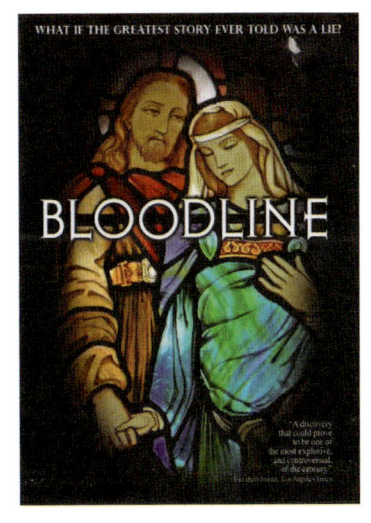

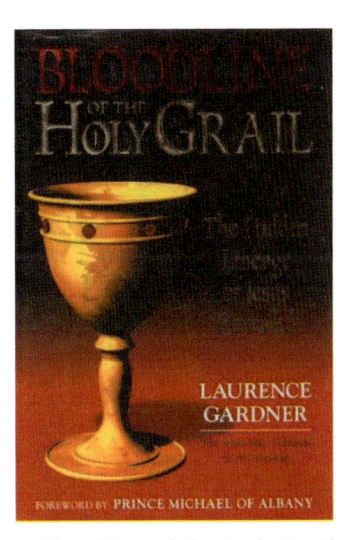

Bloodline   *Bloodline of the Holy Grail*

79

In September 33 AD the first child of Jesus and Mary Magdalene was born. It was Tamar, the Sarah, the princes. Sarah being a title. Also in September Simon Zelotes (Lazarus) was appointed "father" of the Essene community. And Jesus was admitted to the "priesthood", a ritual that was known as "going to heaven". So Jesus became a priest-king and thus part of the order of Melchizedek (Michael-Zadok). According to the strict Jewish law sexual relations were, after giving birth to a daughter, only permitted after three years. So in December 36 AD the marriage was "re-consummated" and in September 37 their first son, Jesus II was born. After the birth of a son they had to live a celibate life for 6 years! What a terrible time that must have been. In December 43 AD they met again and Mary Magdalene became pregnant again.

I must say that all this seems a bit strange. I cannot imagine that Jesus and Mary Magdalene, being so much in love and living so close together, would wait 6 years before resuming their sexual relationship. Besides sex was very important to them. It was sacred and enabled them to gain important spiritual insights and to reach for Heaven.

In September 44 AD their second son was born. He was called Josephus, after his grandfather. Their eldest son, Jesus II, was nominated crown prince in Corinth in 53 AD when he was 16 years old. There he received the title "Justus" and succeeded his uncle Jacobus Justus or Joseph of Arimathea as next in line for the Davidic succession. In 62 Joseph of Arimathea was forced to flee Palestine, see chapter 9. He went to Gaul first to meet up with Mary Magdalene in the Provence. The whole south of France was called the "Provence" at that time. And then went to England.

In 66 AD fighting broke out in Palestine. The Jews captured Jerusalem and held the city for 4 years. But in 67 AD a large Roman army arrived, led by general Titus, who later became emperor. After years of fierce fighting Jerusalem was captured and the Temple of Solomon was destroyed. Only the western wall, the Wailing Wall was left standing.

The Temple of Solomon

All the temple treasures were taken, including the Menorah (or a copy of the Menorah, since the "original, the real" Menorah was not supposed to have a solid base with drawings) and carried off to Rome.

Copy of Menorah   *The real Menorah*

The inhabitants of Jerusalem who had not been able to flee the city were either murdered or sold as slaves. It was the beginning of the "Diaspora".

The Romans persecuted the descendants of the Holy Family, being the children of Joseph and mother Mary and their families, with a vengeance being the children of Joseph and mother Mary and their families. They destroyed all archives, parchments and scrolls relating to the genealogy of David. This was done to avoid later references to the documents and claims to the throne of Israel. The writer Julius Africanus was the first to call the descendants of the Holy Family "Desposyni", a name that stuck.

Tamar was married in Athens, in 53 AD to St Paul. The marriage of Jesus Justus was described as the "wedding of the lamb" (*Revelation 19:7-9*). The lamb can be seen in many drawings and paintings such as here in the church of St Vincent in the town of Carcassonne.

The Last Supper with Lamb

The terms "Word" and "Lamb" were used to indicate the offspring of Jesus. The son of Jesus II, Jesus III was born in 77 AD and was called "The Alpha and the Omega" (*Revelation 21:16*). It is interesting to see that many of the "things" that we were not supposed to know, or where the Church gave out different stories, dogmas and other fairy tales, were actually mentioned in the Bible itself, such as the brothers and sisters of Jesus, his marriage to Mary Magdalene and the children and grandchildren of Jesus and Mary Magdalene.

It is also interesting to see that the Church acknowledged Jesus as being born from the line of David while at the same time proclaiming his virgin birth.

Jesus is said to have died in 73 AD. At that moment his eldest son took over (see *Revelation 22:16*). Mary Magdalene is said to have died in 63 AD in Aix-en-Provence. The old name for Aix is "Acquae Sextiae", after the hot springs of this beautiful city. Mary Magdalene was also called "La Dompna del Aquae", mistress of the waters.

When Jesus was admitted to the Order of Melchizedek his line became one of Priest-Kings. Also called Fisher-Kings. The female line was known as "The Family of the Water", or "The House of Acqs". The male line was known as "Anfortas", meaning power.

The female line was very much present in Aquitaine. From that line stemmed the Merovingian's, the counts of Toulouse and Narbonne and later the kings of Septimania. With a branch to the dukes of Burgundy. So Godefroy of Bouillon, the first "King" of Jerusalem, although he himself did not use that title was, after the capture of the city in 1099, indeed the "rightful" King of the Holy Land.

The Desposyni were at certain times severely persecuted. Especially when the emperors were afraid that they would claim the throne of Israel again. In 208 AD almost 19.000 Christians, Nazarenes, were killed in the area of Lyon.

BLACKENING THE NAME OF MARY MAGDALENE

There are three different persons called Mary Magdalene's; and Jesus. The historical persons as they are being discovered now. Using modern technology, C-14 dating, newly discovered documents and scientific research. Then we have the Jesus and Mary Magdalene as described in the bible. And finally the Jesus and Maria Magdalene as "painted" by the Church. The image of Mary Magdalene in the Bible is not bad. Not bad at all. She is mentioned several times, all in a positive way, a clear sign that her presence was too important to be ignored or left out. She is the woman who was always in the company of Jesus and provided for him. She is the one listening to his stories while her sister Martha is busy serving the guests. She anoints him twice. For what reason is not made clear. She is supporting his mother and his sisters. She is present at the crucifixion. She is the first person to meet him at his open grave.

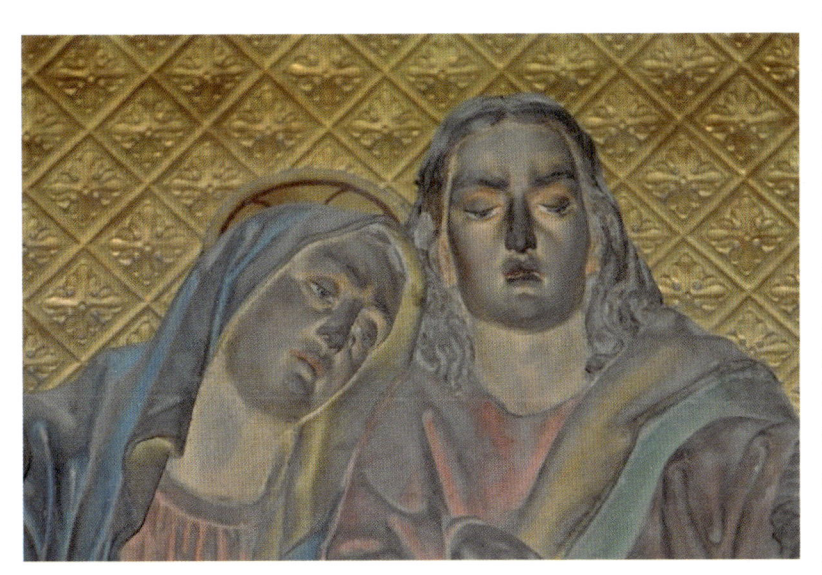

Mary Magdalene comforting Mother Marie

The process of "blackening" Mary Magdalene and with her every woman in Western Europe, began later. But it was done with a vengeance. By pious Church Fathers and Popes mainly in the fourth, fifth and sixth centuries. And it continued well into the twentieth century. In the "Gnostic Gospels", the gospels that surfaced in 1945 in Nag Hammadi, in the Death Sea Scrolls that were discovered in 1947 in Qumran, and in documents discovered in abbeys, universities and private collections, we find a different Mary Magdalene. Different from the woman painted by the Church. Here she was the woman who "Knew the All".

The woman who was his blessed companion, the woman Jesus loved more than all his disciples. His trusted companion. The one who initiated him in ancient mysteries. The "apostle of the apostles" as Hippolythus, the second century church father called her. The one whom he kissed regularly on … …… We don't know exactly where he kissed her, because that word was missing in the parchment, but it seems likely that it was the mouth. But that too is being contested. As everything that deviates from the official "Roman Catholic party line" is contested by the Church. Often so fiercely that one cannot help but believe that it must have been true.

Where did it all start? Where did it go wrong? Where did true Christianity loose its footing? Well, almost immediately. Even before the crucifixion. By the Jewish priests, with their strict adherence to the law, their male, dominating attitude and their avarice, being the rich fruits they collected from the temple. They were the first to condemn Jesus, his pure teachings and his liberal views. They wanted him dead.

Next the Romans, who after the crucifixion, systematically persecuted the bloodline of the Holy Family and destroyed the temple in Jerusalem in 70 AD, causing the infamous "Diaspora".

With the apostle Peter who was jealous of her relationship with Jesus. And who could not stand that a woman was smarter than he was. Peter who even threatened Mary Magdalene. See the knife he is holding in the fresco of the Last Supper, painted by Leonardo Da Vinci. And here in Aurrillac, there are even two knives are on the table, pointing to Jesus and Maria Magdalene.

Peter and the knife

Jesus and Mary with knives, Aurrilac

With Paul who, after a miraculous "intervention" by Jesus, introduced his own version of Christianity to the Greek and Roman world. Paul who was also not particularly fond of women. With the renegade Jewish commander Josephus Flavius, who gave his "own", Romanized, version of what happened in Palestine during the first century AD.

And with some of their disciples who fled Jerusalem after the crucifixion, fearing for their lives. Understandably, but not very brave. Dispersing over the ancient world. Where each fraction developed his own version of Christianity. Resulting in more than 60 different gospels at the start of the fourth century. And not only did many of the gospels differ from each other, some plainly contradicted each other. Several Christian factions were fighting among themselves. No wonder emperor Constantine decided to put an end to this. Besides, he needed their support in his struggle for the imperial crown of the whole Roman Empire. And by that time, we are talking about 315 AD, Christianity was the most popular and most widespread religion in the western Roman Empire.

The emperor wanted one simple religion, a state religion. He called it "Christianity", and it was, officially, based on the teachings of Jesus. But it incorporated quite a few aspects of other, then popular beliefs.

Christianity as we know it today was basically construed during a series of tumultuous conventions during the fourth century, where lots of arbitrary decisions were taken. There it became a state religion. And it was further "adjusted", or augmented, during the following centuries by several, sometimes very curious, papal decisions and dogmas.

At the same time, and this continued well into the twentieth century, Mary Magdalene was marginalized and vilified. Not at first. Not during the first centuries. Then she was held in high regard, being the apostle among the apostles. And being, in my view, responsible for the enormous growth of Christianity, or better said esoteric or Gnostic Christianity, in France during the first centuries. And not in the bible either. Where she was always mentioned with respect, but where it was not always clear 'who was who' and 'what was what'. Pope Gregorius the Great however made in 591 AD a huge contribution to the confusion about who was Mary in the bible. And effectively started the blackening process of Mary Magdalene, by stating that there were several Maries. The one who was a repentant sinner; the one who anointed Jesus and Mary of Bethany and the woman where seven demons were driven out.

Sacred Virgin Mary

But most of all, by linking her to the seven major sins, being pride, jealousy, greed, lust, anger, avarice and laziness. He did an excellent job of putting Mary Magdalene down and with her all the women in Western Europe.

With Mary Magdalene out of the way, tainted and dishonoured, the Church had to find another woman to take her place. After all half the population of the earth consisted of women. So Mary, the mother of Jesus, was selected. Born again. But with her perfect life, her virgin birth, her ascent to heaven and the many miracles attributed to her, she was out of reach of the common people. No one could relate to her. No woman could identify with this godlike creature. She was too sacrosanct.

This is how the once powerful female base, the base of Mary Magdalene and all the women who supported Jesus, slowly died out. And with her the incredibly important feminine part of Christianity and the equally important participation of women in the Church. Lost was the divine feminine. Lost was the Universal Love. Lost were intuition, moderation, creativity, humaneness, and spirituality. No more sacred sex where women could heal and inspire their men. Gone was the Holy Spirit, the feminine part of the Holy Trinity. Forgotten was the ancient, Mother Goddess.

Gone were the power and the wisdom (Sophia), the true compassion, and the moderating influence of women. Gone were the forces of harmony. What a sad, sad loss. And how dearly we paid for that during the next 15 centuries!

Mary Magdalene by El Greco, Montserrat – The power

Mary Magdalene and Seven Sins, Glastonbury

86

THE POWER OF THE CHURCH

But the Church did more than blackening the image of Mary Magdalene. They renounced their Christian origins. They renounced the original teachings of Jesus and Mary Magdalene. They made Jesus into the Son of God. They invented his immaculate conception. They denied that he had brothers and sisters. They denied that he was married and had children. They made him ascend bodily to heaven after he died. And then they declared that his Mother Mary was also immaculately conceived and had also ascended bodily to heaven!

They concocted a new religion, a state religion, intended to keep the people under control. They added malignant concepts like original sin, eternal guilt and penitence. They fabricated a religion full of doctrines, prohibitions, regulations and dogmas. They even invented the "Hell", pictured here in the cathedral of Narbonne.

The "Hell", Narbonne

They "killed" the female Goddesses and all that they stood for. They founded a Church with a strict hierarchy, a Church that positioned itself between the people and God. They based their religion on a book with the supposed words of God, which they called the Bible, written in Latin. A book incorporating various aspects of other, popular religions. A book that the common people were, at first, not even allowed to read! And they did more than that. Much more. They persecuted their fellow Christians. Think of the Albigensian crusade against the Cathars, the persecution of the Knights Templar, the Papal Inquisition, the Religious Wars and the terrible witch hunts.

The Gnostic gospels are the gospels that were not incorporated in the Bible. In total, at the beginning of the fourth century, there were more than 60 gospels. Only 4 of them were chosen for the New Testament. Four gospels were, according to Iraneus, bishop of

Lyon in 180 AD, more than enough. There were, after all, also only four directions of the compass. And we should keep things simple.

One Church, one belief.

Later, even these four gospels were tinkered with. The rest of the gospels was banned, declared forbidden literature and burned, including the Gospel of Philip and the Gospel of Mary Magdalene. Incredible.

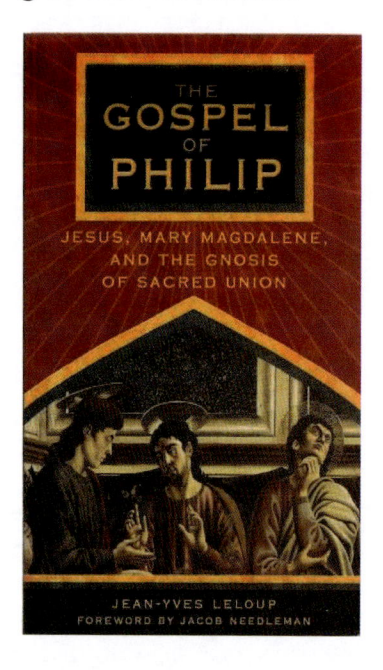

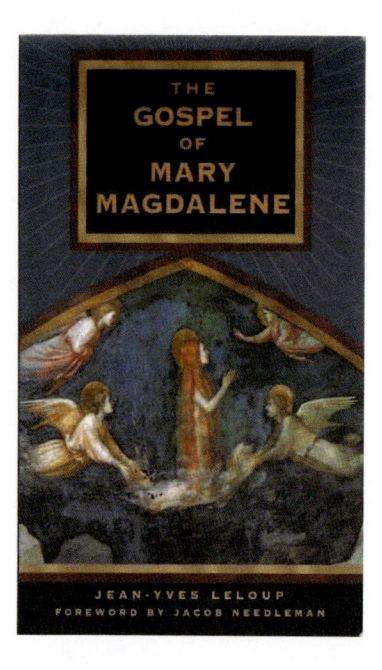

How is it, for heaven's sake possible that these gospels, almost overnight, became heresies! Heresies, the words of Christ, becoming heresies! It is hard to believe.

All this was decided, as we have seen, in a series of tumultuous councils during the 4th century. There was a lot of resistance from powerful and highly respected church fathers. But the line of the emperor, supported by force, prevailed. After all this new religion was not meant for the benefit of the people. It was a power tool for the emperors, and later for the Pope. An effective and convenient set of teachings and dogma's, aimed at keeping the people under control.

In later centuries possession of one of the forbidden gospels, was enough to be condemned to death! In Roman times the Christians were persecuted, a fact that cannot be denied. But they were not persecuted very forcefully, unless their actions were detrimental to the divine authority of the emperor. Later the persecutions were good promotional stuff. Think of the scenes were helpless women were tortured or whole families were devoured by lions. They were the new martyrs, having proved the strength of their faith. But from the 5th century onwards the "new" Christians, meaning the Christians who believed every word written in the "new" Bible, began to persecute their fellow Christians. People with only slightly different ideas. The persecutions were carried out with a vengeance. Incredible. What about Christian love, tolerance and compassion? The new Christians, and especially those in authority, were no Christians at all. They were worse than the Romans. But there is, of course, no mention of these persecutions in any of our history books. Not a word.

And should you think that the power of the Church is diminishing, then think again. Indeed the Inquisition itself no longer exists, but the Institute lives on, be it under a different name. It is being called *"The Congregation for the Doctrine of the Faith"*. And was headed by the present Pope Benedictus XVI, formerly called Joseph Alois Ratzinger.

And as recently as 1950 Pope Pius XII declared that the belief in the Assumption, Mary's (the Virgin Mary) Bodily Ascension to Heaven, was Dogma. Meaning we just had to believe it. And one more thing. When Graham Phillips wrote his famous, or infamous, book The Marian Conspiracy, stating that Mother Mary was buried on the Wales' Island of Anglesey, the book was put on the Index. The list of books forbidden by the Vatican. And it worked. Even in England. The book was officially withdrawn from the Timberland Regional Library.

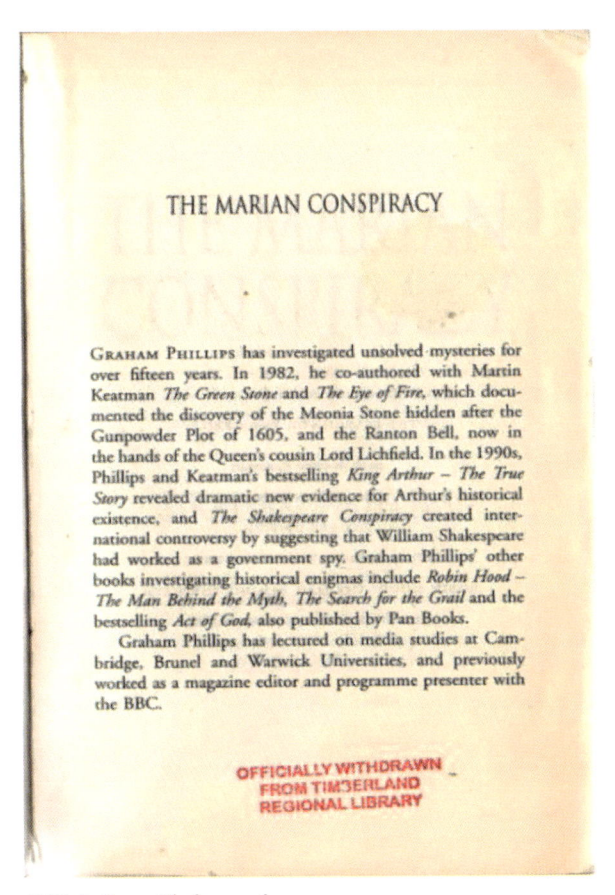

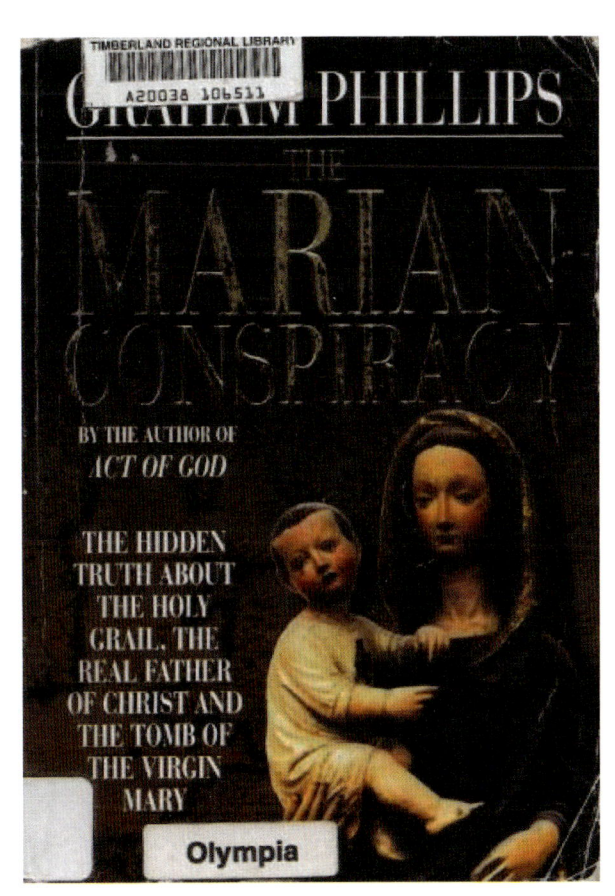

Officially withdrawn!   *Marian Conspiracy*

THE CATHARS

Christianity, by which I mean Esoteric Christianity, Gnostic Christianity, the original teachings of Jesus and Mary Magdalene, was almost completely destroyed in the aftermath of the fourth century. After a series of councils where a new religion was established, based on a new "New Testament" and new Church doctrines. But the original teachings of Jesus and Mary Magdalene were so powerful and so wonderful that they could not be wiped out completely. They survived in the hearts and the minds of the people of Southern France. And resurfaced again when the Church, the Roman Catholic Church, had lost most of its credibility. In their strive for material gain, secular power and doing about everything the Church itself had forbidden. They surfaced in Catharism.

So a second wipe-out was called for. A clean and forceful wipe-out. For Catharism was fast gaining ground. Not only in the Languedoc, but also elsewhere in Europe. In Lombardy, Flanders and Germany. This wipe-out took place during the Albigensian Crusade (1209-1229). It was meant to stamp out Catharism once and for all. It was a ruthless campaign ordered by Pope Innocentius III on June 24th 1208, the name day of John the Baptist. A brutal, religious crusade where more than 100,000, some even say 300,000 and I have even heard the figure of half a million Christians were killed. Many of them burned alive. This picture illustrates both the pureness and sadness of the Cathars, and their friends the faudits, who were slaughtered so brutally. Fortunately Pope John-Paul II apologized in 2000 AD for this outrage.

After 750 years. In memory of the Cathars

The "religious" Albigensian Crusade, of good Christians against bad Christians, or rather the other way round, was followed by the French King, conquering most of the Languedoc, mainly the lands belonging to the count of Toulouse. This campaign was followed by the Papal inquisition instituted by Pope Gregory IX in 1233, further enslaving the people of the Languedoc.

We don't know much about Catharism. Only a few documents survived, such as the anonymous document *"Heresy Catharorum Lombardia"*, and the documents *"Summa de Catharis et Pauperibus de Lugduno"* by Raniero Sacconi and *"Tractatus de Haereticis"* by Anselmus of Alexandria. All other documents were destroyed by the Church. Most of what we know now comes from their adversaries. From the missionaries sent out by the Pope to persuade the 'heretics' to return to the "true" Faith. And of course from the interrogations performed by the Inquisition. Well known are the reports of Bernard Gui from Toulouse, Jaques Fournier from Pamiers and Geoffroy d'Ablis. The reports from Jaques Fournier, who later became Pope Benedictus XII (1334-1342), were the basis for the historical novel *"Montaillou"* written by Emmanuel Le Roy Ladurie.

Catharism is a dualistic religion. A religion of good and evil. Light and dark, body and spirit. Differentiating between the immortal soul and the mortal body. Cathar reasoning is as follows. How is it possible, that evil came into this world if God is only goodness and love? There must have been, next to God the creator of the spiritual world, the world of light and beauty, a second God, the creator of the material world. The world of materialism, power and flesh. This God was known as Yahweh, Satan, or the Demiurge. The God of the Old Testament, the God who rules over a depraved, materialistic world. A vengeful God.

The idea isn't new. There had been other dualistic religions, like Mazdeism with the prophet Zoroaster, who preached more a way of living then a religion. People should have good thoughts, speak good words, and do good things. By living a good life they would get closer to God. Catharism is a Gnostic religion. Gnostic meaning "knowledge". It is a religion aimed at enlightenment, at personal growth, at gaining knowledge, at spiritual growth. It is a religion of direct contact with God, the creator of the spiritual world, a religion of love and wisdom.

No so long ago people thought that Catharism originated spontaneously in regions like the Rhineland in Germany, Lombardy in Italy and the Languedoc in France. Regions that were prosperous, where women were respected, regions that knew a certain amount of religious freedom and were reasonably tolerant. They thought that Catharism was a natural reaction to the corrupt and power hungry Church. A Church of fear, sin, penitence, dogmas, indulgences and excommunication. The church that was doing nothing for her believers. A Church that had positioned itself between God and the people, where priests were striving for material gain and where bishops, cardinals and popes were striving for secular power.

Others thought that Catharism had come gradually to these regions. Originating in the Middle and Far East, from religions like Mazdeism, Buddhism and Hinduism and then slowly spreading to the West, creating religious trends like Manichaeism (3rd century AD), Paulicians (6th century AD) and Bogolism (10th century AD).

Some people think otherwise, including me. I think that Catharism is, and was, a continuous, Gnostic undercurrent. A current that was kept alive through the ages because the message was so good, so clear and so powerful, and because the preachers were so passionate and

The beauty of Mary Magdalene

so sincere. The lived the life they preached. The people, who had listened more than a thousand years ago, to the teachings of Jesus and Mary Magdalene, treasured these messages. They were messages of love, of hope and of understanding. Messages that touched the soul. Messages that were embedded in the hearts of the people, in spite of all efforts of the Church to stamp them out.

Many of these messages were contained in the more than 60 Gnostic writings scorned by the Roman emperors and the early Church fathers. They were the gospels that were not selected for the New Testament during a series of unruly conventions in the 4th century AD. Fortunately the Roman Catholic Church was, at least until the Albigensian crusade and the Papal Inquisition, not very powerful in the Languedoc. The Languedoc was a region that knew powerful rulers like Alaric the Visigoth, Clovis and Dagobert I and II the Merovingians, Charlemagne the Carolingian and the Kings of Septimania – rulers who did not care much for Rome and did not easily bend to the will of the Church.

Catharism sprang, in my view, and I know this is subjective, but it is my view, a feeling from the heart, from the seeds sown by Mary Magdalene in the south of France. A similar process took place in England, where Joseph of Arimathea preached the teachings of Jesus, resulting in Celtic Christianity, a much more Gnostic and "natural" religion than the orthodox teachings of Rome. In later centuries the English monarchs and priests clashed regularly with Rome. There was always friction between Rome and England – over issues as Pelagianism, disputing the rightful succession of the popes in Rome, over Thomas à Becket who refused to acknowledge the law of the King in crimes committed by priests, over the Dissolution Act of Henry VIII, disbanding all abbeys and cloisters, frustrated as he was by the arrogance of the Church and the refusal of the Pope to annul his first marriage, finally resulting in the establishment of the Anglican Church.

What did the Cathars believe? Or rather what did they not believe? Well, they didn't believe Jesus was the Son of God. They didn't believe in the virgin birth. They didn't believe he died on the cross. Jesus was a prophet, yes, and a teacher, a very important teacher, showing the people the way to enlightenment and reminding them of their divine nature. They didn't believe in the original sin. Jesus didn't come to free the people from their sin, but from their ignorance.

They didn't like the Church as an institute. The Church with her relics, her saints, her sacraments. To say nothing of its infamous trade in indulgences or their excommunication practices. They did not accept the celebration of the Eucharist. How could bread and wine turn into the body and blood of Christ? They didn't believe in Heaven and Hell, or in the Last Judgment. Hell didn't exist, unless it was the imprisonment of the divine spark in every human being in his or her physical body. They believed in reincarnation. Each life on earth was a step towards enlightenment. By living in poverty, love and compassion, never using violence or lying to other people, they hoped to get closer to God, their Spiritual God. Their religion was not based on the Old Testament, but on the New Testament and mainly on the Gospel of John and possibly on the forbidden Gnostic Gospels of Thomas and Philip as well.

There are scholars who think that Mary Magdalene wrote the Gospel of John, and that John the beloved disciple was none other than Mary Magdalene, the dearly beloved disciple. They think that John was invented by the Church to get Mary Magdalene out of the way. This idea was strengthened by the many "curious" changes that were introduced in the Gospel of John – changes that only prove that the Church wanted to hide something. And often the effort to hide things is the best way to attract attention. The attention they just wanted to avoid. The Gospel of John, or Mary Magdalene, is also the most trustworthy gospel. It reads like an eyewitness's account. And what better eyewitness than Mary Magdalene?

Christian Doumergue, a highly respected French writer and "connaisseur" of Mary Magdalene devotes a whole chapter to John the beloved disciple versus Mary Magdalene in his book *"La Terre Elue"*, the Chosen Land. Illustrating the confusion between John and Mary with many pictures where John the beloved disciple has unmistakable female characteristics.

There are also writers who think that John the beloved disciple was Lazarus. The only male who was explicitly called "beloved" by Jesus. Some take this one step further and think that Lazarus was homosexual. That being the reason why he was leaning so often, so close to Jesus. But all this is speculation. It makes much more sense that Mary Magdalene, who was clearly loved by Jesus, was the beloved disciple. Or that she was "John" the beloved disciple. That it was she, sitting next to Jesus and leaning towards him. And that she wrote the Gospel of John. The only gospel that was read by the Cathars. The Gospel they always carried with them.

The word "Cathar" means pure or clear. There were different "grades" in Catharism. The "Auditeurs" were the people who listened to the message of the Cathars. The "Croyants" were the believers. At the height of Catharism about 50 % of the population was said to be "believers". The "Chrétiens" were the priests, those who had received the "consolamentum", the sacred blessing. They were later called "Les Parfaits", "the perfect ones", by the Inquisition. A name that stuck and was carried with pride. The local people called them "bonhommes" and "bonnesfemmes", meaning good men and good women, for men and women were equal in the eyes of the Cathars. Men and women could both be priests. And very good priests they were. They lived an exemplary life. The parfaits were highly respected. They were skillful craftsmen, good weavers and excellent healers. They had to and wanted to, for they worked for their living.

The parfaits are said, for example by Antoine Gadal, to have undergone a severe training. Some say this training took place in the Holy Mountain in Ussat-les-Bains. A mountain full of caves and tunnels. Even now the caves are very impressive and carry a special atmosphere. Eerie sometimes. I have visited the caves many times, guiding people around. And every time my friends got there, they were very quiet, impressed. Or scared and crying. Some of the caves are huge, like the Hermit cave.

The sacred mountain in Ussat-les-Bains

The Hermit cave in Ussat-les-Bains

Not as big as the Lombrives cave on the other side of the river Ariège, but still huge. Some caves are highly energized, like the Eglise cave. Or are filled with happy energy forms, high frequency energies called Orb's, like the Bethlehem cave.

The Bethlehem cave full of Orbs   *"Energised" cave*

There was also a Cathar church. But this was nothing like the Church of Rome. It had not even a special building. And certainly nothing resembling the magnificent cathedrals, basilica's and churches built for Rome. Churches blinking with gold, "received" from grateful and fearful believers. No, the Cathars met in the houses of the people, the houses of friends, or out in the open. Just like Jesus did. There was no hierarchy and there were no relics, statues or other artifacts.

The Cathars believed themselves to be the true successors of Jesus and his disciples. They "operated" in exactly the same way. The Cathar church had no managerial or hierarchical function, but a spiritual one. The Cathar bishops initiated their parfaits by the ritual of consolamentum. An initiation or baptism performed by the laying of hands on the head. The parfaits obeyed strict rules: no earthly possessions, no intercourse, no meat or cheese, eggs and butter. No killing of men or animals, not even in self-defense and always telling the truth. No financial support, no taxes, only gifts and legacies. In 1226 there were 5 bishops in the Pays Cathare.

It's not so difficult to see what danger Catharism constituted for the Church of Rome. It was different, pure and inviting. And their religion was spreading. The Roman Catholic Church tried, it really tried – that must be said – to bring the Cathars back to "true" Christianity. But to no avail. The differences in belief systems and attitude were too great. After all these efforts it needed only a single incident to spark the wrath of Rome. On

January 14th of the year 1208 AD, the papal envoy Pierre de Castelnau, who had terribly misbehaved in Toulouse, was murdered in St Gilles du Gard – probably by a soldier of the count of Toulouse, who was however far too clever to have ordered such an act. The furious Pope Innocent III then called for a crusade against the Cathars – on June 24th, the feast day of John the Baptist. He excommunicated all Cathars and all those who helped them, including Raymond VI count of Toulouse and Raymond-Roger Trencavel, viscount of Carcassonne. Being excommunicated meant being labeled "outlaws'. And outlaws, even Christian outlaws, could be killed without committing a Christian sin! How convenient.

A huge army was assembled at Lyon. Some say 300,000 men. Some were knights, some were clergymen and the rest were brigands, bandits and ruffians. They had all received forgiveness from the Pope for their previous sins! Yes, the ways of the Church are at times incomprehensible. The Albigensian crusade had started. The crusade was officially led by the papal envoy Arnaud Amaury, who later became the fanatical archbishop of Narbonne. Simon the Montfort was the military leader. It would turn out to be an incredible cruel and brutal crusade, a crusade of Christians against fellow Christians. Some even called it genocide. Simon the Montfort was so feared and so hated by the people of the Languedoc that even now hardly any new born baby is called "Simon".

On July 22nd 1209, the feast day of Mary Magdalene, the city of Béziers was conquered. Everybody was killed, more than 20,000 people. Including seven thousand people seeking refuge in the "Eglise Madeleine" and in the cathedral. They were all killed. The churches were set on fire. The papal envoy Amaury, when asked how to discern between true Christians and Cathars, is said to have answered: "Kill them all. God will know his own." It was the day when the Church lost the respect of its people. Not their power but their respect.

Béziers

After that Carcassonne and Toulouse were taken. The country was plundered and devastated. More than 400 villages were burned. Hundreds of people were mutilated or burned at the stake. In 1210 AD 140 Cathars died at the stake in Minerve. A dove hewn in the rock still reminds us of that horrible fact.

And in 1211 AD 400 Cathars were burned alive in Lavaur. Another dove hewn in rock reminds us of that atrocity. I will not recount the whole gruesome scenario of the Albigensian crusade, with its kings, its counts, its popes, its bishops, its battles, its treason, its changing alliances, its treaties, its convictions and its cruelty. It is too horrible to contemplate.

Dove of Minerve

Dove of Lavaur

Just a few highlights.

In 1229 the treaty of Meaux, near Paris was concluded, officially ending the Albigensian crusade. However, not being able to fully eradicate Catharism from the "Pays Cathare" Pope Gregory constituted in 1233 the Papal Inquisition. A more horrible institution can hardly be imagined. The task of finding and persecuting the heretics was given to the Dominicans. They were first responsible to the bishops of the diocese where they operated. But when some of the bishops protested against the cruelty and the indiscriminate torturing and killing of innocent people, the Dominicans answered only to the Pope. Where upon all hell broke loose.

However the actions of the newly installed Inquisition were so brutal that the country revolted. New armies were assembled, new alliances were formed. But it was too late. The Albigensian crusade, which started as a religious war, had now become a secular war, with the King of France

Castle of Montségur

participating in the campaign and occupying the lands of the count of Toulouse, comprising roughly the present day Languedoc.

The castle of Montségur became the official seat of the Cathar church. It was especially fortified. The Montségur was the only "Cathar" castle that was fortified. All the other Cathar castles, now famous tourist attractions, were built in the 10th and 11th century by local warlords. They were however gratefully used by the Cathars as places of refuge. Montségur was called by many names, like the Vatican of the Cathars, the Grail castle, the Temple of Light, the Pyramid of the Pyrenees and many others.

In 1243, siege was laid to the last fortress of the Cathars, the famous Montségur. The head of the Cathar dragon had to be cut off. There was fierce resistance from the soldiers defending the castle. And the fortress was practically impregnable – until the water supply was poisoned. Negotiations about surrendering the castle were started. The castle would be surrendered on March 16th, 1244. All who renounced Catharism would be spared. In the two weeks before surrendering the castle, special ceremonies were held. So special were they that several soldiers converted on the spot to Catharism, knowing full well that a certain death awaited them!

On the night before the surrender four Cathars left the castle. They silently descended the mountain, taking with them the most precious treasure of the Cathars. Nobody knows what that treasure was, surely not gold or precious stones. The Cathars didn't care for material wealth. It could however be the location of their 'treasure' for they had gathered quite a lot of money, meant for sustaining the defense of the Montségur and for buying off the victims of the Inquisition. Gold and silver would be far too heavy to get them safely down the steep rock.

It could have been "The book of love", a supposedly heretical booklet written by Jesus or Mary Magdalene. It could have been documents proving the marriage and genealogy of Jesus and Mary Magdalene. It could have been the knowledge that Jesus and Mary Magdalene were deeply in love with each other and were married. And had children. It could also have been any of the forbidden gospels. Maybe even the second gospel of John, the beloved disciple. Or the "*Cène Secret*", the most treasured secret book of the Cathars, "Cène" meaning the last supper. Or special rituals and ceremonies. Or sacred numbers and symbols. Or documents proving the true origins of Catharism. Maybe even the sermons of Mary Magdalene herself.

All highly explosive material at that time. And even now, in this time. We don't know what the "treasure" was. It could even have been the knowledge stored in the heads of the parfaits themselves. The treasure was never found. And no one knows where the four parfaits went. Some say to Spain, to Montserrat, others to the initiation caves near Tarascon-sur-Ariege. Others say they went to Limoux or to Rennes-le-Château.

On March 16th 1244 some 225 Cathars were burned alive in the field at the foot of the 'Pog' of the Montségur. In 1960 a memorial stone, a stèle, was placed at the site of the field. Written on this monument was the text: "To the Cathars, to the martyrs of the pure Christian love, 16 march 1244".

If you climb the Montségur, it takes about half an hour and is something of a pilgrimage, then please stop at this memorial and stay there for a while.

The Monument at Montségur

Think of all the Cathars who died there, singing. And lay a flower, a rose, at the monument. The field where the 225 Cathars were burned, is now full of flowers as often happens on places where terrible things took place.

Fields at Montségur

In 1244 one hopeful statement was made. It said that in 750 years' time, the laurel would blossom again on the Montségur.

But it did not end at Montségur. The last castles to fall were Quéribus and Puilaurens. Still, in the remote areas of the Pays du Sault, catharism survived for several more decades before it was stamped out by the Inquisition. The last perfect to die was Guillaume Bélibaste, born in Cubières, not far from Bugarach. He was burned at the stake in 1321 near the castle of Villerouge-Thermenès.

Quéribus

And now the Laurel blooms again, literally and figuratively. For Catharism is alive. Very much alive. It is like a religion reborn. Thanks to some dedicated French scholars. Now there are museums, magazines, bookshops with hundreds of books, magazines and beautiful pictures of the Cathar castles. Thousands of tourists visit the Pays Cathare each year. "Cathar" has become a brand name in the Aude department. With Cathar restaurants where plenty of wine and meat is served! With Cathar accountancies, Cathar garages and even Cathar undertakers!

Just south of the city of Narbonne an impressive monument has been erected, dedicated to the memory of the Cathars. It is located along the AutoRoute des Deux Mers, the road that leads straight into the 'Pays Cathare'.

Monument at Narbonne

Catharism is a religion reborn. Maybe it is still the same, continuous Gnostic undercurrent that surfaced in the time of the Cathars. A religion that is surfacing again in our time. Just in time to save the world. This pure and Gnostic religion is "calling out" to more and more people. It is as if "l'Histoire se repète", as if history is repeating itself, as if this beautiful religion is replacing the old and outdated doctrines of the Church of Rome and the conservative protestant churches. For Catharism represents the original message of Jesus and Mary Magdalene: a message of love, enlightenment and spiritual growth. A message to take to the heart. No more striving for power and materialism. We have had enough of that.

The twentieth century was the most violent century in living memory. But now, now that we have found our freedom, the heritage of Jesus and Mary Magdalene and the heritage of the Cathars, is coming to the surface again. Now we can create a new religion, with Catharism as a wonderful model. For we all long for the return of universal love and sacred femininity, for harmony between the sexes, for female priests. For churches preaching the original message of Jesus, like in the time of the Cathars. We long for a religion that teaches us respect for nature, for each other and for Mother Earth.

Lavaur near place where 400 Cathars were burned alive in 1211

This picture taken a Lavaur, close to the place where in 1211 more than 400 Cathars were burned alive, is a powerful reminder of the anguish of the people who died there.

THE KNIGHTS TEMPLAR

In 1095 AD Pope Urban II held a council in Le-Puy-en-Velay, discussing the possibility of launching a crusade against the Holy Land. "Deus lo volt" he said, "God wants it" or "God wills it." He was supported by the influential Cisterciencer monk Bernard de Clairvaux , who later became the "Auctor Intellectualis" of the founding of the Knights Templar.

Bernard de Clairvaux

"Deos lo volt", God wills it...

The story of the Knights Templar is closely related to the story of the crusades. Not the Albigensian crusade, but the crusades to the Holy Land. Why exactly the crusades were undertaken is still a mystery. There are several possibilities. Was it because the Muslims had conquered Jerusalem? It is possible, but not very likely. For that happened in the year 638 AD. And since then, at least most of the time, pilgrims from the west were allowed to visit the holy city. Was it because the Byzantine army had been beaten severely by the Muslims in 1071 AD and emperor Alexius I of the East Roman empire had asked the Pope for help in defending his empire? Was it because the Franks and Byzantines were not allowed to enter the Syrian harbours in 1093 AD? Or was that just an incident?

Was it because the Pope, Urban II wanted to re-establish his authority after his long struggle for power with the German emperor? Or was it because the Church of Rome had lost much of its credibility and prestige in their continuous strive for material gain and secular power? The priests and bishops were by now so corrupt and so focused on material matters, that people no longer feared the Church. Or was it because many young, French noblemen, with nothing better to do, were up to all kinds of mischief and were fighting amongst each other? Or was it because the Church needed a common, external enemy to overcome its internal problems? Or was because in abbeys, or at the courts of Flanders, Champagne, Bourgogne, Lorraine and the Languedoc interesting information had surfaced., pointing to Jerusalem. To extremely valuable treasures buried under the Temple Mount. Or was it all of that? Well it probably was.

Pope calling for Crusade, Clermont-Ferrand

What happened was that in 1096 the first crusaders, a collection of peasants, adventurers and a few knights, left for Palestine. They were slaughtered in Hungary and in Turkey. The regular armies, in total consisting of 60,000 men, and led by capable and important noblemen, fared better. They left a year later. In 1097 Nicaea in Turkey was conquered, and in 1098, after a long siege, Antioch was captured.

On July 15th 1099 Jerusalem fell. A terrible bloodbath followed. A shame to the Christian armies. Half the population of the Holy city was murdered. The streets were like rivers of blood. After that the love between Muslims and Christians was gone forever.

In 1118 AD a group of nine knights, led by Hugues de Payens, a member of the count of Champagne appeared before King Baldwin I in Jerusalem. They said they were soldier-monks. Their task was to keep the roads free of brigands and to

The City of Jerusalem

protect the pilgrims. A pretty tough job I would think, for only nine men. The knights were lodged in a wing of the palace of the King, on the exact location where once the Temple of Solomon stood. They stayed there for nine years, not taking part in any battles, but steadily digging under the Temple Mount. Traces of their activities were found by Sir Charles Warren who conducted excavations under the temple in 1860 AD. The knights returned to France in 1127. At the Council of Troyes in 1128 Bernard de Clairvaux, one of the most influential persons in Europe, called for the establishment of a new order, the "Ordo Pauperum Commilitonum Christi Templique Salomonici".

The Order of the Poor Knights of Christ was established on January 17th 1128. After this event Hugues de Payens traveled through Europe asking the royal and noble houses for money and land with incredible success. No one knows why so many noble houses gave so easily so much money and so much land to this new order. And why so many knights joined the order. There must have been a very good reason for that, something to do with the "Arc of the Covenant" or other treasures?

In 1139 the Pope issued a bull stating that the Knights Templar only needed to swear allegiance to the Pope and were exempt from paying taxes. Again a highly unusual decision.

A Knight Templar

That is the official story. Now let us go back to the court of the count of Champagne. The count was a very powerful man, a descendant of the Merovingian kings and thus of Jesus and Mary Magdalene.

Since 1070 an influential school flourished in Troyes, the capital of Champagne. By the way, the oldest church in that city was dedicated to Mary Magdalene. People studied the Kabala and other esoteric documents at his court. It was "early renaissance time" in Champagne, as in other regions like the Languedoc, Lombardy, Flanders and Burgundy. It is quite possible that new documents came to surface in that period. Or that new translations were made from Arabic, Greek, Aramaic or Hebrew documents. Or that old, hidden documents surfaced from the archives of abbeys, churches and royal courts.

We know that new documents were also imported from the East or were acquired from the Moors living in Spain. People were no longer afraid of the Church. And they were longing for knowledge. There might also have been rumors, from pilgrims who had traveled to the Holy Land, of hidden treasures in Jerusalem. They might

Church of Mary Magdalene, Troyes

even have found another copper scroll, like the one found in Qumran in 1947, naming 60 different locations where temple treasures were buried by the Jews. Some say that a passage in the Talmud, the holy book explaining the laws of Israel, stated that a treasure of incredible value was hidden under the Temple Mount. We know that the count and some of his noblemen talked at length, in 1104 AD, with one of his knights who had just returned from Jerusalem. What did that tell them? What had he found? We don't know. But we know that the count himself, shortly afterwards, went to Jerusalem, where he stayed from 1104 until 1108 AD. Something that looked very much like a reconnaissance mission.

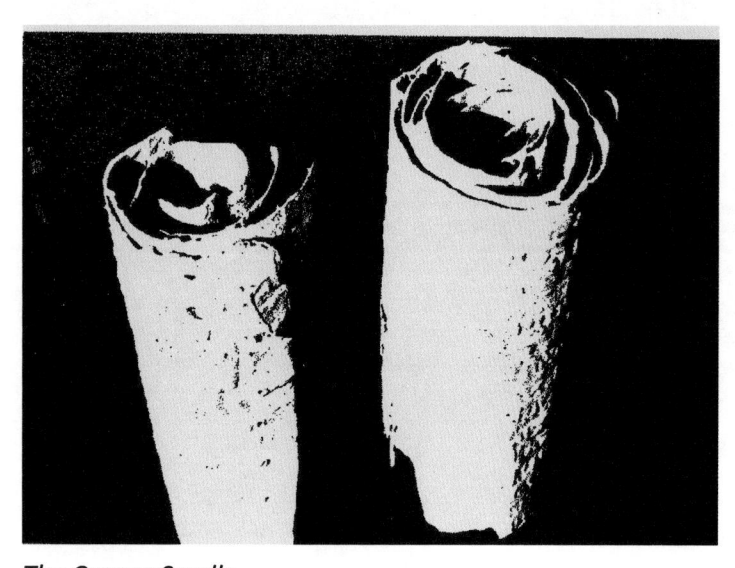

The Copper Scrolls

The count returns in 1108. But shortly after his return he goes back to Jerusalem. In 1108. To what purpose? To discuss with King Baldwin I the possibilities of a group of knights staying at his palace and digging under the Temple mount? Quite possible. A year later he is back in France. Why? To get a group of trusted knights together? To prepare for the establishment of a new Order, the "Milice de Christ?" Or the secret Order of the Priory of Sion? An Order of highly influential men who were to stay in the background. The "Godfathers", so to speak, of the Knights Templar. That too is possible.

In 1215 the count granted a large piece of land to the Order of the Cistercians. Where Bernard de Clairvaux would later build his famous cloister of Citaux. Why did he do that? To gain the support of Bernard de Clairvaux and through him of the Pope? The thing is that from the year 1115 onwards, serious money began to flow back from Palestine to France. Lots of money. Where did that money come from? We don't know, but we do know that the Cistercian Order grew explosively. Within 50 years more than 300 new abbeys were built. The crusaders and more specifically the Knights Templar brought untold riches from the Holy Land back to Europe.

What were the Knights looking for? Well there are several possibilities. First of all the temple treasures hidden by the Jews before the destruction of the Temple by the Romans in 70 AD. Then the 64 locations where treasures were hidden as described in the copper scrolls of Qumran, discovered in 1947. The most likely option however is that they were looking for the Arc of the Covenant, the most treasured relic of the Jews. The passage in the Talmud probably referred to this most sacred object. The Arc of the Covenant was not heard of or mentioned since the 7th century BC. It seemed to have vanished. The Arc is pictured, on wheels, on the porch at the north side of the Cathedral of Chartres. Maybe the Arc was hidden in a secret chamber under the Temple Mount, just before the Babylonians conquered Jerusalem in 587 BC.

Arc of the Covenant, Brenac

Maybe it was hidden somewhere in the desert near Mount Nebo or in one of the many caves of the ancient city of Petra, in present day Jordan.

The Arc of Convenant, Chartres

Petra in Jordan

Maybe it was brought to safety via the Temple of Elephantine in Egypt and an island in Lake Tana to the Beate Mariam church in Aksum, in present day Ethiopia. And maybe it was brought to safety in the new Temple of Salomon under the Pech Cardou in France. It could also have been taken by the Babylonians and destroyed. But no record exists that they took the Arc, while all other captured treasures were described in detail. But there are more possibilities. It is possible that the Knights Templars actually found the Arc of the Covenant under the Temple Mount. Or that they found documents telling them where the Arc was hidden. Or that they found an empty Arc. Or that they recovered the Arc from Aksum, with the help of the banished Abyssinian prince Lalibela, using an expeditionary force to force their way in and bring the Arc back to Jerusalem. There are stories that the Templars were planning to build a special church in Jerusalem to house the Arc of the Covenant, in the Holy City, where it belonged. However by that time the Holy Land was seriously threatened by the Saracens. So the Arc was brought to safety in France, the Second Holy Land, where it could have been hidden in different places, among them the Pech Cardou. There are also stories that the Arc was moved several times, from one location to another. One of the reasons being was that the "energy" of the Arc was so strong that people could not bear it for any length of time. Then they went mad.

The Saracens recaptured Jerusalem in 1187. Several researchers have stated that the power of the Arc was not so much due to the Arc itself, as well to the content(s) of the Arc. That could have been the stone tablets received by Moses, or the emerald stone from the crown of Lucifer, or a special meteorite. Others say that the Arc contained the Holy Grail. Or that the Arc of the Covenant and the Holy Grail were the same. But let's not talk about the Arc of the Covenant, but about Mary Magdalene, and about the teachings of Jesus.

108

The Knights Templar must have discovered, apart from the Arc of the Covenant (with or without the Holy Grail) many other interesting items in the Holy Land. Treasures, High Tech knowledge, alchemical processes, the origins of Christianity, the secrets of the ancient religions of Egypt, India and Mesopotamia, highly sensitive documents, "explosive" secrets, genealogies, forbidden gospels, the "truth", the historical truth, about John the Baptist, Jesus and Mary Magdalene. Things that had been buried for ages by the Church. Or where different explanations, read dogmas, had been forced in place.

Within 20 years the Order became incredibly rich and extremely powerful. From 1240 AD onwards more than 80 cathedrals and 70 churches were built in that graceful, new Gothic style. Buildings conforming to the rules of the Golden Mean, a feast for the eye. Like the cathedral of Chartres. All financed by the Knights Templar. Some say that the cathedrals and abbeys were also built according to special ground patterns. Conforming to the "As above, so below" rule, reflecting on earth the star constellations in heaven. See the book *On Earth as it is in Heaven*, by Greg Rigby. All these churches and cathedrals were originally dedicated to Mary Magdalene.

The Cathedral of Chartres

The fight in the Holy Land went well, at least in the beginning. Under the kings Baldwin II and III new territories were conquered. But from 1140 onwards things started to change. In 1146 Bernard de Clairvaux called for a second crusade in Vezelay. It was no great success. In 1169 the Egyptian Vizier Saladin joined the battlefield and in 1187 Jerusalem was conquered by the Moors. From 1189 until 1270 six more crusades were launched. With as one of the "highlights" the fact that in 1204 the city of Byzantium (Constantinople), on request of the Doge of Venice, was conquered and plundered by the crusaders, resulting in the final separation of the Western and Eastern Churches. From 1216-1221 the 5th crusade took place, ordered by

Aigues Mortes

Pope Innocentius III who was now conducting two crusades at the same time. One in the first Holy Land, Palestine and one in the Second Holy Land, the Cathar country.

In 1229, after the 6th crusade, Jerusalem was handed back to the Christians for a period of 10 years. Then the Christians were beaten in 1244 in Gaza. The 7th crusade was launched in 1248 from the fortified city of Aigues Mortes. It was led by King Louis IX, later called Louis the Saint.

His statues can be seen all over the south of France.

The last crusade took place in 1270. It was a disaster. The huge fleet of the crusaders, led by Louis the Saint, was enclosed in the harbor of Tunis. Many died, including Louis, because of the foul air. Finally in 1291, the last bastion, Accra, fell. It was the end of an era. The next centuries saw a reversal on the battlefields. Turkish armies conquered large parts of Eastern Europe. They even came up to the gates of Vienna.

What was the relationship between the Cathars and the Knights Templar? We are not sure, but we think that most Templars sympathized with the Cathars. They did however not take part in the fight. They had sworn a vow not to take up arms against fellow Christians, irrespective of their excommunication. I wish the Pope had made such a vow! The Knights Templar were very powerful, especially in the south of France. They owned large pieces of land. About 1/3rd of their properties were situated in the Languedoc. That region almost became a Templar Kingdom in its own right.

Louis the Saint, Aigues

Bertrand the Blanchefort, one of the grandmasters of the Knights Templar, invited in 1156 a group of German miners and metal workers to Rennes-le-Château.

Chateau Templiers

They started digging in Rennes-le-Château, Rennes-les-Bains, Montferrand and Blanchefort. In gold and silver mines that had long been exhausted. Why? Maybe to hide something or to look for treasures? To find the entrance to the Temple of Salomon? We don't know. There were many Templars in the Rennes-le-Château area. In Alet-les-Bains alchemical experiments were carried out. Campagne-sur-Aude was an important administrative center. And of course on the "Chateau Templiers", formerly called Chateau d'Albedun was an important Templar commandery. From the chateau one has a magnificent view over the area, covering Rennes-le-Château, Bugarach and the road from Carcassonne, via the Col de St Louis, to Perpignan. However on Friday October 13th 1307, still considered to be an unlucky day, all Knights Templar in France were apprehended, as ordered by King Philip IV, with the full knowledge of Pope Clement V.

John the Baptist with his finger

But the fabulous treasures of the Knights Templar were never found. Most probably the Knights were forewarned and had carried their treasures to safety. To Portugal, Scotland or even North America. What were their treasures? Gold and silver, coins, certainly, but there was more. The knights were deeply involved in esoteric activities. Something that was later so vehemently denied that it had to be true. Was it the Arc of the Covenant, the stone of Lucifer, the elixir of life, the genealogy of Jesus and Mary Magdalene, the head of John the Baptist or their knowledge of ancient religions, sacred geometry, alchemy and astronomy? Or all of it?

We know that the Knights Templar were great admirers of both John the Baptist and Mary Magdalene. And that they protected an "explosive" secret. A secret that had to do with Mary Magdalene. A secret known only to a few Templars and Cathars. The men at the top. A secret never revealed, not even under the harshest tortures. In my view the Templars in Jerusalem had found information referring back to the Languedoc. Maybe to the Temple of Solomon, to the Arc of the Covenant, to the marriage of Jesus and Mary Magdalene or to their tomb under the Pech Cardou. For people wanting to know more about these fascinating subjects I advise the books of Lynn Picknett and Clive Prince, among them "*The Templar Revelation*".

The Templars had a high regard for women. In the beginning women were even admitted to the ranks of the Knights Templar. This woman in a shop in Carcassonne might have been one of those Templar women Later this was forbidden.

Templar woman at Carcassonne

The Templars honored a skull, like this one above the entrance of the cemetery at Rennes-le-Château. We don't know whose skull it was, probably from a woman. It could have been the skull of Mary Magdalene. The skull was apparently called "Baphomet", which people thought had something to do with the devil. But according to the Atbash code, a secret code used by the Knights Templar for their trading activities, Baphomet was the code name for Sophia, meaning "wisdom". And Sophia was closely related to Mary Magdalene and the ancient Goddesses Isis, Artemis and Diana. And to the sacred marriage, Hieros Gamos. And the emerald stones of Hermes Trismegistos, stones that were said to contain all the wisdom of the ancient world. We don't know, but it is likely that the secret of the Knights Templar, (and the Cathars) had to do with ancient wisdom, with special knowledge, with John the Baptist, with Jesus and Mary Magdalene and with sacred femininity.

Cemetery Rennes-le-Chateau

Another secret of the Templars was the process of producing one atomic gold powder, white gold, called Ormus, which was used in stained glass windows to give them an uncanny brilliance. It was also an important ingredient for the elixir of life. We think that this white gold powder was produced near the Chateau Templiers, situated between Rennes-le-Château and Bugarach.

THE HOLY GRAIL

The Grail is not a Christian invention. It existed long before Christ. Some 4,000 years ago is was something that came from the Gods. A medium, a vessel to communicate with the Gods. Later the content of the vessel became more important. When you looked into it or drank from it, the most wonderful things happened. As if some kind of transformation was taking place. The Grail also provided worldly and spiritual nourishment. Civilizations from the first millennium BC saw the Grail as a kettle, a cauldron.

A kettle in which the Gods had mixed the elements of creation. From where the cosmos was born, from where humanity was created. The word "Graal" was used for the first time around 1200 AD. Together with the sudden appearance of the Grail legends.

The Grail as cauldron

A few years later, as might be expected, the Holy Grail was "claimed" by the Church. It became the cup used at the Last Supper, it represented the Eucharist mystery, or was the jar that caught the blood of Christ hanging at the cross. And it could also have been the alabaster jar, used to anoint Christ, like this cup seen in Broceliande in Bretagne.

The Grail is usually depicted, by the Church as a golden chalice. To be seen in many churches, often on the ceiling, in the South of France. But what is the Grail? Let me give you a brief overview of what it could be. The goblet or cup used at the last supper, to drink the wine or to represent the mystery of the Eucharist. The cup or cruets used to catch the blood of Christ or his blood and sweat, while hanging at the cross. Although I think it highly unlikely that Mary Magdalene or any other person, would actually be standing under the cross to catch the blood and sweat of Jesus. Or a stone. The stone of

Grail in Broceliande

wisdom or the stone of the alchemists. Or a meteorite falling from heaven. See the book *"When the Gods came down"* by Alan F. Alford. The emerald from the crown of Lucifer. Or an incredibly powerful crystal, a crystal that influenced everyone in its vicinity.

Maybe it was a platter, with wonderful dishes, carried by two virgins in the castle of the wounded Fisher King. Or a plate with the head of John the Baptist, or even a phallus cut off from the body. Or the cauldron of Geridwin with plenty of food and drink. Where warriors who were killed in battle could be revived again. Or the famous Blue Bowl found on Beckery Island and now kept in the Chalice Well Gardens in Glastonbury.

Or one of the crystal skulls, originating, they say, from Atlantis. Skulls that are now being reproduced in great numbers and are used for special ceremonies Maybe the Grail stood for secret knowledge, knowledge concerning sacred geometry, special initiations, or the secrets of the Universe.

Or special knowledge, solis sacerdotibus, only for the initiated. Or maybe crucial knowledge for mankind. Knowledge enabling us to survive future planetary disasters. Or objects that gave the people incredible power.

Ceiling in Brenac

Goblet used at the last supper

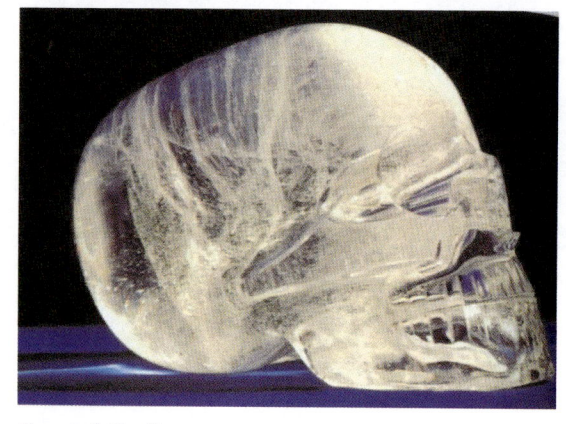

Crystal Skull

Alabaster Cup of Mariam

But could also have been the bloodline of Jesus and the bloodline of Joseph of Arimathea. Or the Holy Family itself with their offspring, the Desposyni. Or the unborn child of Jesus in the womb of Mary Magdalene. It is interesting to see, as mentioned before, how many statues of Mary, the Church says Mother Mary, but I think Mary Magdalene, show a woman who is clearly pregnant. See [chapter 17](). Maybe the Grail is the Black Madonna, La Vierge Noire, so popular in France and Catalonia in Northern Spain. It could even be the divine spark inside of us, locked up in our human body. Longing for reunification with our Divine Creator.

Others see the Grail as the female principle, or as sacred femininity, or as the strive for harmony between the sexes, between our male and female energies. Or maybe it is the sacred marriage, the Hieros Gamos, where the woman, the Goddess, makes her man into a King. Where the people are happy and where the country prospers. Or the elixir of life. A drink containing the famous white gold powder, Ormus, or according to other writers, a mixture of snake poison and blood. Or was it the cup of Marian, discovered by the empress Helena, the "Marian Chalice", so vividly described by Graham Phillips in his book *"The Chalice of Magdalene"*, The search for the Cup that held the blood of Christ. Or sacred objects like the lance ,Longinus, of Petronius or the sword that cut off the head of John the Baptist, or a bell made by King Solomon, or the portrait made by Nicodemus, the "Volto Santo".

Painting of the Volto Santo

Although the statue of the Volto Santo in Lucca, Northen Italy, looks a bit different.

Volto Salto statue, Lucca

The Grail in Rennes-le-Chateau

Maybe the Grail looks like this goblet at the foot the Calvary in the garden of the church on Rennes-le-Château.

Maybe the Holy Grail was Mary Magdalene herself. No one else possesses so much of the Grail characteristics. The sacred marriage, the child in her womb, the bloodline of Jesus, secret knowledge, magical powers, initiation ceremonies. She had the power to inspire her man, by sacred sex and special rituals. She was the carrier of the alabaster jar used to anoint Jesus, twice. She held the cup used at the last supper and the cruets used to catch the blood of Jesus. She was and is the symbol of sacred femininity, of equality and harmony between men and women. She is the apostle of the apostles, the bringer of good news. She is the personification of the lost teachings of Jesus. For me the Holy Grail is real. It is a wonderful treasure. And that treasure is Mary Magdalene. She has it all. She is the lover, the partner, the mother, the companion, the teacher. She has the knowledge, the compassion, the beauty, the magic, the inspiration and the love. Look at her, this beautiful woman, with her alabaster jar in the Hostellerie of La-Ste-Baume.

Mary Magdalene in Hostellerie Ste. Baume

Strange things have happened to the Grail and the Grail legends. This sacred object had not been mentioned anywhere when suddenly, out of the blue, the Grail Legends appeared, all in a very short period of time. What happened? How is it possible that between 1190 AD and 1220 AD, eight different Grail stories were produced? Well, there may have been several reasons. For these were turbulent times. Many expected that in 1000 AD or else in 1033, a thousand years after the death of Christ the world would perish and a new Kingdom would come. When that didn't happen, the people lost heart and the Church lost some of its stature. Then an early Renaissance started in regions like Champagne, Flanders, Burgundy, Lombardy and the Languedoc. New ideas, new values emerged. And in 1056 the duke of Normandy, William the Conqueror conquered England. And did everything he could to establish his lawful right to the throne of England.

At the end of the 11th century the crusades began, resulting in new views on Christianity, ancient religions, John the Baptist and the historical Jesus and Mary Magdalene. There was an exchange of ideas and knowledge between Muslims and Templars. New, sacred knowledge was acquired, valuable documents, manuscripts and relics, like the Black Madonna statues, were taken to Europe. Stories about the Arc of the Covenant and the Holy Grail surfaced. Money was pouring in from Palestine. New churches and cathedrals were being built. Catharism was flourishing. Mary Magdalene came out of the shadows. All perfect ingredients for the Grail Legends.

The first Grail legend was called *"Peveril or La Folie Perceval"*, by the monk Blayse. Writing about the descendants of Joseph of Arimathea and four sacred Grail attributes: the cup, the sword, the plate and the lance.

Many of these symbols can be seen on a rock drawing in the "Grail castle" of Mont-Real-de-Sos, near Tarascon-sur-Ariege.

Grail castle Mont-Real-de-Sos

Grail Drawings

Then came "*Le Conte del Graal*" by Chretien de Troyes, who got his story from the Count of Flanders. With Perceval as the leading part. Describing the Grail as a dish of pure gold inlaid with precious stones. Next the two *"Continuations"*, featuring first Gawain and a dish full of food and then the Volto Santo, a wooden portrait of Jesus made by Nicodemus and left by Joseph of Arimathea in Lucca in Toscane when he traveled to the White Land. The land located somewhere in Great Britain, most likely Wales. Next *"Joseph d'Arimathie"* written by Robert de Boron, the most popular of all the Grail stories. The Grail was the cup used at the Last Supper, the cup with a few drops of the blood of Jesus. Handed to him by the resurrected Jesus when Joseph was in prison, where Jesus told him secret of the Eucharist.

Then *"Didcot Perceval"* in French prose, by an anonymous writer. Describing the adventures of Perceval. Watching in the castle of the Fisher king, protected by Arthurian warriors, a procession of beautiful maidens, carrying the Grail. And failing, at first, to ask the right questions. But coming

Grail procession

back later and inheriting the Grail after he did indeed ask whom the Grail served. Next *"Parzival"* written by Wolfram von Eschenbach. He describes the Grail as a stone, a magic stone, fallen from Heaven. With incredible powers. Anfortas the king of the Castle, protected this time by the Knights Templar, is wounded but cannot die because of this stone. Parzival, the son of his sister Herzelyde, again fails to ask the right question. But later he returns, asks the right questions and succeeds his uncle. Then *"Perlevaus"*, a French Grail legend by an anonymous author. He claims the story is translated from an old Latin document kept in a sacred house on the Isle of Avalon. Perceval succeeds where Gawain failed and sees the Grail in a small chapel, together with the skull of John the Baptist, a bell made by King Solomon and several other relics.

Finally the Vulgate Cycle, written in plain language. Consisting of two stories, *"Lancelot"* and *"Queste del Saint Grail"* written by anonymous Cistercian monks. The first story, describing the Grail as a small booklet written by Jesus himself. Later the story is infused with Christian elements and the Grail is said to be a cup.

A few hundred years later all these stories culminated in the famous *"Le Morte d'Arthur"* by Thomas Malory. Adding however nothing new to the previous legends. Then there is another story, written by Klaas van Urk, a Dutch author. He thinks the Grail legend is a description of the epic voyage of a small army of Knights Templar to Abyssinia. Where they captured the Arc of the Covenant, and brought it back to Jerusalem, from where it was later transported to France. What do these Grail legends tell us? Is it about the bloodline of the Holy Family, the desposyni? The descendants of the Fisher King? Or about Mary Magdalene carrying the child of Jesus in her womb. Is it about the Arc of the Covenant, or the stones that fell from heaven? Stones with incredible power. Is it about knights gaining knowledge and wisdom on their travels through the country? Or about the lost teachings of Jesus, the lost Gnostic Christianity and the barren land. Or is it about the lost Sacred Feminine. Or is it still the cup used at the last supper. I don't know. But for me Mary Magdalene, and all she stands for, comes by far the closest to the Holy Grail.

Mary Magdalene in the cave of la Ste. Baume

BLACK MADONNA'S

Around 1200 AD, many of the now famous Black Madonna's, or Black Virgins surfaced or resurfaced. Discovered, most of the time, by simple peasants in caves, in trees or buried deep in wells. Black Virgins were adored and highly respected by the local people, because they represented the Mother Goddess, and all the other powerful Goddesses like Isis, Artemis, Diana and also Mary Magdalene.

Isn't it strange that Mary Magdalene is so clearly associated, in the minds of the common people, with the Black Madonna's while the Virgin Mary, the supreme Christian Goddess, is not? Does this mean that we unconsciously differentiate between the powerful ancient Goddesses and her 'artificial' substitute introduced by the Church. Could it be that the statue of Mother Mary with the child Jesus on her arm, statues that can be seen in every Christian church, were the answer of the Church to the statues of the Black Madonna's? It might be worthwhile to investigate in what period the statues of Mother Mary with Jesus on her lap, first appeared. And what the major differences are between these statues and the statues of the Black Madonna's, apart from its color of course.

Diana in Alet-les-Bains

In the 16th century AD, just before the terrible religious wars (1562-1598), almost 200 Black Madonna's existed in France. While in the whole world about 450 Black Madonna's could be found, at least according to Ean Begg in his book *"The Cult of the Black Virgin"*. The origin of the wonderful and awesome Black Virgin statues can be no other than the Goddess Isis with the infant Horus on her lap. And Mary Magdalene can be seen as a "modern" personification of Isis. She radiates the same power, magic, creativity and femininity. Mary Magdalene, a "Christian" Goddess in a long line of powerful Goddesses, like Maat, Inanna, Isthar, Hathor, Lilith, Cybele, Demeter, Athene, Persephone, Aphrodite, Artemis, Diana and many others. All Goddesses; representing various aspects of the power of the Mother Goddess, like wisdom and the power to create, but also to destroy. Representing the power to give life, to love, to make a man into a real man, or even a King.

It is interesting to see that the statues of Black Virgins are not just pretty "dolls" to be admired for their beauty and clothes, but real symbols of power. The people who look at them are often flabbergasted, excited and surprised. I know I am. I stare at them and feel something crawling up my spine, triggering ancient memories. People often stare are them, fascinated, for a long time. Reliving ancient memories. The Black Madonna's symbolize pagan goddess-worship, wisdom, resuscitation of dead babies, the terrifying maw of death from Kali, rebirth, healing power, the female principle, love of the body, a stream of knowledge, astrology, alchemy and universal love.

Kali, Les Ste-Maries-de-la-Mer

The origin of Black Madonna's or Black Virgins is not clear. They are pre-Christian, like the Grail. Coming from Egypt, which means "black". Or from Syria, brought over by Syrian immigrants. They could also have a Celtic origin. It is interesting to see how many Black Madonna's can be found in old, sacred places of the druids, like in Auvergne and the Ardèche. See the famous Notre Dame du Puy in Le-Puy-en-Velay. In fact there are two Black Madonna's in that magic city. One the original and one an exact copy of the Black Virgin burned in 1794 during the French Revolution.

Notre Dame de Puy   *Copy of Notre Dame de Puy*

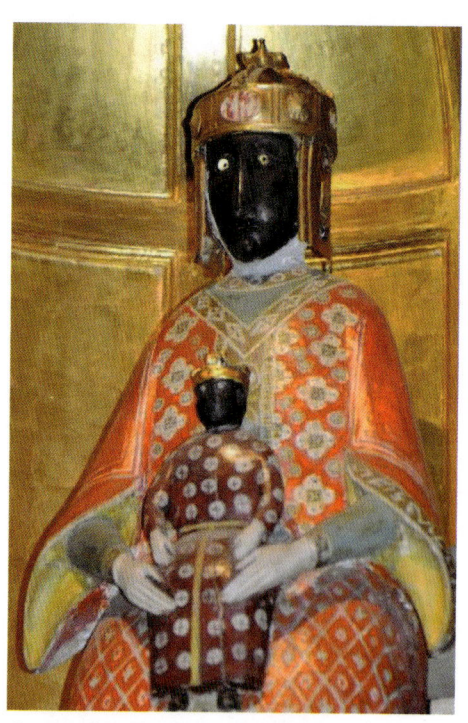

Others state that the Black Virgins originated in Merovingian times, roughly between 500-750 AD. Like the famous statue of the Notre Dame de Boulogne. According to ancient traditions one day in the year 633 or 636 AD, during the reign of King Dagobert I, a boat without oars, sails or crew, entered the mouth of the river Liane, where now Boulogne-sur-Mer is located. Carrying a statue of the Lady of Boulogne and a copy of the gospels in Syriac.

In 888 AD, not long after the liberation of Barcelona, the dark Madonna of Montserrat, now lovingly called "La Morenata", was discovered by shepherds in a mountain cave where a Gothic bishop had hidden her from the Moors.

Notre Dame de Boulogne *La Morenata in Montserrat*

Most of the Black Madonna's however were "discovered" in the early Middle Ages. And the cult of the Black Virgin is essentially a product of the 12th century Gothic renaissance. A time when the Knights Templar returned from the Holy Land. Bringing with them all kinds of treasures, like (possibly) the Arc of the Covenant, religious artifacts like (possibly) the original Menorah, statues of Black Madonna's, precious documents and sacred knowledge about alchemy, astrology and sacred geometry.

The Black Virgins brought back from the Holy Land, or rediscovered in springs, tree trunks or caves, were placed in newly built cathedrals, churches and chapels. Buildings that were erected on top of old sacred places. A good example is the Cathedral of Chartres, with her two Black Madonna's. Built over an ancient well. A sacred place of the Druids.

The Lady of the Pillar and the Lady of Under Ground. There is even a Blue Virgin in the stained-glass window. All vividly described by Jean Markale in his book *"Cathedral of the Black Madonna"*.

Lady of the Pillar, Chartres

Notre Dame sous Terre, Chartres

It is wonderful to see that many Black Madonna's were found by simple folk, like peasants, fishermen, farmers, sailors, shepherds. And sometimes even by cattle. As vividly illustrated by the stain glassed window in the Notre Dame du Cedon. Or by the horse of Charlemagne after he returned from battle in Spain. As can be seen in the Notre Dame de Sabart near Tarascon-sur- Ariège.

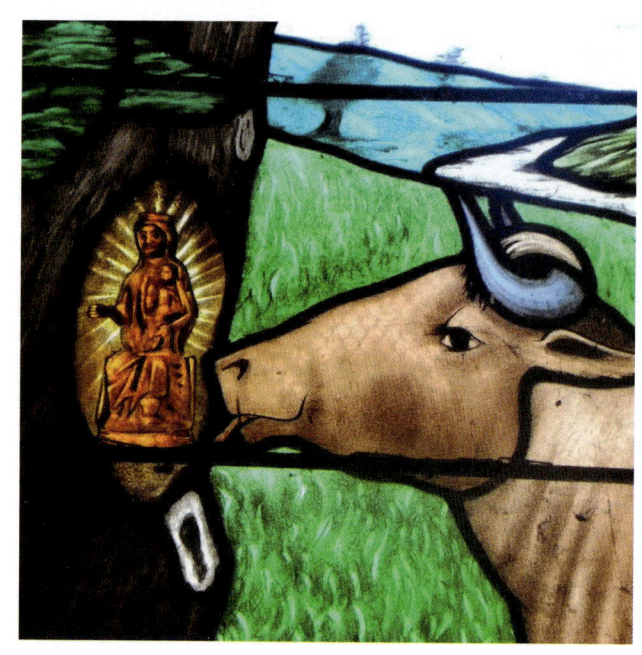

Notre Dame dus Cedon

Notre Dame de Sabart

Notre Dame des Miracles, Orléans

They were found in old and sacred places. In caves and springs, in the roots of trees, on the crossroads of ley lines, in open spaces in the woods or in places with a special energy. The common people loved these images. They meant a lot to them. The statues protected them in times of war, and from the plague and other disasters. There are many stories of Black Virgins being carried around the town to ward off evil. And it worked, it often worked. A good example is the Notre Dame des Miracles in Orléans, a church dating from the 5th century, where the Black Madonna, brought by Syrian Immigrants, has "performed" several miracles. In 1221 the statue extended her leg and thus caught an arrow in her knee, meant for one of the most important defenders of the city. Joan of Arc prayed to her on May 8th 1429 after freeing the city from the English. And during the bombardments by the Germans in June 1940 the tower and the sanctuary housing the Black Madonna were spared, while the rest of the church was in ruins. Another example can be found in Verviers, Belgium, where in 1692 hundreds of people witnessed a miracle. During an earthquake the child of the original Black Madonna turned towards his Mother.

The people respected their Black Virgins and honored them. And resisted any change in their appearance. It is wonderful to see with how much courage, ingenuity and tenacity the people were striving to hide, save and preserve their precious Madonna's. During the wars of religion, the French Revolution and the Spanish Civil War. It did not always work, but several times it did.

The original Black Virgin, *Verviers*

The Child turned, Verviers

Why was she black? People often wonder why the Madonna's were black. The "official' explanation by the Church is that they were blackened by the smoke of burning candles. That is nonsense of course. For their clothes and the other statues in the vicinity, were not affected by the smoke. If the Black Madonna's were blackened at all, it was by the Church. For the Church did, and I suppose still does, not particularly like Black Madonna's. The statues represent old Goddesses, female power, sexuality and love. Subjects not really favored by the Church. And the statues often referred to pre-Christian times, to Merovingian secrets, to Catharism and to the Knights Templar. Also subjects not very popular with the Church.

There has always been some confusion as to why the statues are black. Some say it is the material, black stone. But most of the statues are made of wood. Others attribute the blackness to deities like Isis, Mary the Egyptian, Sarah the Egyptian maidservant, or the Queen of Sheba who said "I am black, and I am beautiful, O ye daughters of Jerusalem", one of the most famous texts from the Song of Songs. Black was also the color of wisdom. And women were, and still are in my opinion, much wiser and often much more religious than men. And the priests and priestesses of the Nazarenes wore black cloaks as well.

The attitude of the Church towards Black Madonna's has never been very positive. If they could not destroy the holy places where they were found or where they stood, they would "Christianize" them. They would build chapels, churches, basilicas or even cathedrals on top of them. Or they would erect an altar dedicated to the Virgin Mary on the same spot.

They often rededicated the temples housing Black Madonna's, to Mary the Virgin, like the temple of Diana in Le Puy, where now stands this huge, 16 meters high statue of the Notre Dame de France. Similar actions were taken at the temple of Isis in Soissons and the temple of Cybele in Autun.

Notre Dame de France in Le Puy-en-Velay

Notre Dame de Fourvière

Notre Dame de Murat

And in Lyon with the chapel of Thomas a Becket next to the famous Notre Dame de Fourvière. With two Black Madonna's. On top of the chapel again stands a huge golden statue of the Virgin Mary. And in Marseille with a magnificent golden Virgin Mary on top of the Notre Dame de la Garde, also housing a beautiful Black Madonna. And in Murat where on top of the hill overlooking the Notre Dame de Murat a huge white statue of the Virgin Mary is located. All very impressive power play by the Church.

Often the Church replaced the statues with those of the Virgin Mary with the infant Jesus. Stating a little later that these statues had been those of the Virgin Mary all along! Or they simply ignored them. Many of the statues disappeared over time, were desecrated, stolen, or damaged. Even in 2009, the famous Black Madonna in the Notre Dame de Marseille near Limoux, 20 kilometers north of Rennes-le-Château, was stolen. One year later it was replaced by a new Black Virgin, but this statue didn't "radiate", it had no "soul"

Original Notre Dame de Marceille

New Notre Dame de Marceille

Where in France do we find Black Virgins? And what is their relationship to Mary Magdalene and the Mother Goddess? That might be an interesting topic to research. I found that in most, if not all of the Black Virgin sites Mary Magdalene was also present. Not just in the "Stations of the Cross", where she always can be found. But in special chapels, wonderful statues, or beautiful paintings. Like in Le- Puy-en-Velay, Clermont-Ferrand, La Daurade in Toulouse, Rocamadour, in Orléans, in Moulins, the St Victor in Marseille, the Notre Dame de Grace in Honfleur and Boulogne-sur-Mer, just to name a few. Most of the Black Virgins, by far the most, can be found in Auvergne and the Ardèche regions. In Clermont-Ferrand and ancient sacred sites of the Druids, like Le Puy. More can be found in the Bourgogne and Lorraine areas, in the Provence and in the Languedoc. However there are many other, famous Black Virgins in France.

Let's make a quick tour through the Second Holy Country, showing where the some of the most famous Black Virgins can be found. Black Virgins that are still "open" to the public. And I apologize beforehand for all the Black Madonna's not mentioned in this overview. Let's start with the Black Virgin in the ancient basilica Notre Dame de la Daurade in Toulouse, originally representing Pallas Athene, the Goddess of wisdom. And in the same city, the Notre Dame du Taur.

Notre Dame de la Duarade, Toulouse

Notre Dame de Verdelais near Bordaux

Notre Dame du Taur

Next we go to the Black Virgin in the Notre Dame de Verdelais, south east of Bordeaux. Moving to the north to Douvre la Delivrande on the north coast of Normandy and further along the coast to the Notre Dame de Grace in Honfleur. Further north we have the Notre

126

Dame of Boulogne. Going north through the middle of France we encounter one of the most famous sites, the Black Virgin of Rocamadour.

Notre Dame de la Delivrande

Notre Dame de Grace, Honfleur

Rocamadour

And just north of Albi is the famous Notre Dame de la Dreche with two Black Madonna's. Right in the middle of France we find the Notre Dame de Moulins.

Notre Dame de la Dreche 1

Notre Dame de Moulins

Notre Dame de la Dreche 2

Further north there is the Black Virgin in the Notre Dame des Miracles in Orléans. Orléans was since the 11th century an important center of the Ste Mary Magdalene cult. And of course the two Black Virgins in Chartres.

Notre Dame Bon Secours, Metz

Avioth

A little east of Orléans is the Notre Dame the Bethleem, in Ferrieres en Gatinais. A tiny Black Virgin in a very long robe. And let's not forget the Black Virgins in Paris. Continuing our tour clockwise and following the frontier with Belgium we come to the Black Virgin of Avioth, near Stenay and the famous abbey of Orval.

In Lorraine we will find the Black Madonna of Metz, on the site where once a temple of Diana stood. In the cathedral of St. Etienne existed, until the 16th century, a statue of Isis. In Nancy, capital of the House of Lorraine, we find the Notre Dame de Bonsecours on the outskirts of the city.

And in Sion-Vaudemont, on the Colline Inspirée, a nursing Madonna in the Notre Dame de Sien, the patroness of Lorraine. In Bourgogne we will find a Black Madonna in Dijon, in the Notre Dame de Bon-Espoir, on the Zero Meridian of Paris. A Madonna that saved the city from the Swiss in 1513 and from the Germans in 1944. In Baume, between Dijon and Lyon we find a beautiful, multicolored Black Madonna.

Notre Dame de Bon Secours

Notre Dame de Bon-Espoir

Multicolored Black Madonna, Baume

There is also a Black Madonna in Tournus. Then, on top of the hill, looking out over Lyon, we will find the famous Notre Dame de Fourvière, beautifully decorated. Next to the basilica is the chapel of St Thomas a Beckett, housing two Black Madonna's, the Notre Dame de Bon Conseil and a replica of a previous Black Madonna .

Note Dame Bon Conseil, Lyon   *Replica, also in Lyon*

And again to 'top off' these Black Madonna's, and to Christianize them we find on top of the chapel a huge golden statue of the Virgin Mary.

The Virgin Mary on top of the chapel Thomas a Becket in Lyon

In Auvergne we can find many Black Virgins. The most famous are those in Le-Puy-en-Velay, already mentioned and those in Clermont-Ferrand. One in the Cathedral, Notre Dame de Clermont where the priest did not want to acknowledge the statue as a Black Madonna and the other, a beautiful, small statue in the basilica of the Notre Dame du Port. But Black Madonna's can also be found in little villages, like this beautiful Black Madonna in la Chapelle Geneste, near the village of La Chaise Dieu. And the same goes for Mauriac. In the Rhone valley we will find a Black Madonna in Lyon, and in Ay, the Notre Dame d'Ayde, famous for its resuscitation of stillborn children. Further east, near Chambery is the Black Madonna of Myans.

Notre Dame du Port, Clairmont-Ferrand

Notre Dame de Clermont

La Chappelle Geneste

Mauriac

Myans

Chapel of the Notre Dame de la Garde

Notre Dame de la Garde, Marseille

In the Provence Black Madonna's can be found in Aix-en-Provence, in the chapel of La Madeleine and in the famous Notre Dame de la Garde in Marseille. The Notre Dame de la Garde towers high above the harbor of Marseille. On top of the basilica the shining, 9.7 meters high, golden statue of the Virgin with child can be seen. Also in Marseille in the basilica of St. Victor, mentioned before, we find the Notre Dame du St. Victor

More Black Madonna's can be found in the Notre Dame de Confession, in St-Martin-de-Vésubie, near the Italian border, 2000 meters high in the French Alps, called the Madone de Fenestre. Brought there, so they say, by Mary Magdalene. And in Arles, in the Notre Dame de Grâce.

In the Languedoc region Black Virgins can be found in Montpellier, now in the museum and in Pezenas, the Notre Dame la Noire or Notre Dame de Bethlehem. Many more statues can be found in the Pays Cathare consisting of the departments Pyrenees Oriental, Aude, Taur and Ariège. First there is the White Madonna in the Notre Dame du Bon Secours

Notre Dame du St. Victor

in Puivert, although some think that this is a statue of Artemis. Then the Black Madonna in the Notre Dame du Val d'Amour in Belesta . And the Black Madonna in the Notre Dame de Celles.

In Tarasçon-sur-Ariege the Notre Dame de Sabart, with the famous Black Madonna without child. Said to be found by the horse of Charlemagne, when he returned from Spain after doing battle with the Saracens. The stolen and replaced Black Madonna in the Notre Dame de Marceile has already been mentioned.

Notre Dame de Celles

Notre Dame de Bon Secours, Puivert

Notre Dame de Fenêtre, St Martin Vesubie

Notre Dame de Sabart

ND de Bethleem

ND de Sion-Vaudemont

More famous Black Madonna's can be found in the Abbey of St Michel de Cuxa, near Prades, in Prats-de-Mollo, near de Spanish border and in Thuir, a Black Madonna of lead. In Corneilla, the Black Madonna with seven "douleurs", seven swords in her body and in Villefrance de Conflent. And let's also mention the Black Madonna of Nuria in Spain, just over the border, south of Mont Louis. It is the most venerated Virgin of the Catalan Pyrenees. A small copy of the Maureneta from Montserrat can be found in the little church of Montségur flanked by this curious statue of a black Madonna with child.

BV in Prats-de-Mollo   *BV of Nuria*   *Notre Dame de Vie, Villefrance*

BV of Corneilla, with the 7 "douleurs"   *Black Virgin, made of lead, Thuir*

Copy of Maurenata, Montségur

Black Madonna, Montségur

And what is happening now? We are witnessing a strong and renewed veneration of Black Madonna's. The magic statues attract more and more people. It must be slightly uncomfortable for the Church, to see so many people flocking to these Black Madonna's, located in their churches and cathedrals. But this is amply compensated by the commercial value of the Black Madonna's. Very interesting. for the Church and for all the shops in the area selling lots of postcards, mini statues and picture books of the Black Madonna's.

Who are the people that are coming to see these statues?

In my view most of them are looking for their roots, for ancient mysteries, for the magic of the Black Virgin and for the awesome power of the Mother Goddess. I think that the "resurrection" of Mary Magdalene has strongly supported this renewed interest in Black Madonna's. As did the independent position of women, equal to men, in the West, the emancipation processes, the return of Sacred Femininity, and the growing interest in other religions, like Catharism, Buddhism and Gnosticism. They all played their part. We now see a rapid growth of spirituality, of respect for nature. Themes as unconditional love are becoming popular. The books of Eckhart Tolle and Paul Ferrini are selling well. Harmonizing male and female energies, in both men and women, has become an major issue. And the renewed interest for Black Madonna's, and of course Mary Magdalene, fits nicely in these quests.

But still Black Virgin statues disappear. They simply vanish. Or go to museums (Montpellier) where they don't belong. Or to private collections, where they don't belong either. Some priests even have the "courage" to state that the well-known Black Virgins in their communities never existed! Others are being repainted and some are stolen.

Abbey of St. Martin du Canigou

Like the old Black Madonna in the abbey of St. Martin du Canigou, where now only a dull photograph is presented. Some were stolen quite recently, like the famous Black Madonna of the Notre Dame de Marceille, near Limoux. Other, lesser known Black Madonna's, suffer from indifference and neglect by the Church. Or are being subjected to an embarrassed suppression, often disguised as protectiveness. When will they ever learn?

Two more interesting items. In many churches, basilicas and cathedrals we find a Notre Dame. The Notre Dame of the city, or the Notre Dame of Santé, Bon Secours or Bon Espoir. Or other wonderful meanings. It is not always clear if such a "Notre Dame" is a Black Madonna or the Virgin Mary with child. I tend to believe that all the "Notre Dames" are Black Madonna's. Statues with special powers, protecting special places. They often return to the place where they are found or where they are meant to be after being transported to other places. And very often the young child in the lap of the Notre Dame shows a will of his own. Turning away, laughing or holding his hands in a special way.

Notre Dame Du Cros

Captivated by the Black Madonna

Last but not least. Once I went with a good friend to the Notre Dame du Cros near Caunes-Minervois in the Aude. There is a lovely Black Madonna in the church. After leaving the church I lost my friend. I went back in the church and there she was, staring at the statue of the Black Madonna.

Completely captivated and transfixed. She could not move an inch and I had to forcibly remove her from the scene. Such is the power of Black Madonna's.

FAMOUS FACES AND SCENES

Mary Magdalene is no doubt the woman who has been portrayed more than any other woman in the world. Because she is so beautiful. Because she is a woman to whom people, especially women, can relate. Because she is the embodiment of love, suffering, wisdom, sexuality, compassion, joy and spirituality. There are beautiful books portraying her in her different "roles". Three I would like to mention. First of all *"Marie Madeleine ou la Beauté de Dieu"*, *"Mary Magdalene or the beauty of God"*, by Jaqueline Kelen. Portraying her as the beautiful one, the ardent one, the silent one, the ravished one, the dazzling one, the lonely one and the unassailable one. Next *"Sur les pas de Marie Madeleine"*, following in the tracks of Mary Magdalene, by Frederique Jourdaa and Olivier Corsan. And finally *"MARIE MADELEINE, secrets et histoire"*, by Karen Ralls, describing the historical Mary Magdalene, the oriental and occidental traditions, the pilgrims sites, the Vierges Noires and the Alabaster Jar.

Mary Magdalene has been portrayed in many different ways. As the sexually attractive woman, the prostitute, with a beautiful body, bare breasts and long flowing hair. As the repentant sinner, kneeling before Jesus and asking forgiveness for her sins. As the woman from whom seven demons were driven out. As the one who washes his feet with her hair and anoints him for the first time, as seen here in St Gilles. And in Rennes-le-Château. As the beautiful bride, anointing Jesus for the second time with the precious Nardus oil. As the woman who instructs him in the secrets of spirituality and sexuality.

St. Gilles

Rennes-le-Château

Or the one sitting next to him at the last supper, knowing that he will soon be apprehended, tortured and crucified. Or clinging to his feet at the crucifixion, weeping, and full of sorrow for the pain of her beloved. As seen here in Prats de Mollo, close to the Spanish border where Mary Magdalene hides her face.

The Last Supper, St. Volusien, Foix

Last Supper, Prats de Mollo

Softly crying when his lifeless body is taken from the cross as here in Vinca near Prades and in the St. Velusien church in Foix.

Church of St. Volusien, Foix

Church of Vinca

Comforting Mary the mother of Jesus and his sisters at the crucifixion. Being the first to see him after the resurrection, with the famous "noli me tangere" scene. Telling the happy news of his resurrection to the other disciples. Mourning his death, together with mother Mary, in that famous, Pieta scene. And preaching the good news, the teachings of Jesus, to all the people who want to hear her message. Baptizing people.

Abbey of St. Hilaire, Marie with St. John

And last but not least as the woman who was lifted up by angels, seven times a day, to hear the songs of heaven and see her beloved Jesus. Sometimes it is not clear if it is Mary Magdalene who is depicted. Mary Magdalene is often confused with other Maries. Like Mary the mother of Jesus, Mary the Virgin with the roses, or Mary the Egyptian.

Hostellerie la Ste. Baume

Virgin Mary or Mary Magdalene?

Or with her sister Martha in Troyes. And in the chapel of Mary Magdalene in the cathedral of Mirepoix where she could be taken for Mary Magdalene, but where it is clear that she is Martha, when seen together with her sister Mary Magdalene and her brother Lazarus.

Lazarus, Mary Magdalene and Martha in Mirepoix

Martha in Troyes

Sometimes she is confused with other female saints, like St. Lucia who is said to have put out her own eyes to look less attractive. Or with Goddesses like Isis, Artemis, Diana or Venus. And sometimes we see beautiful girls in churches, holding the stoup or standing at the entrance or in the porch. Girls with no names, but who could very well be Mary Magdalene.

St. Lucia  *Bram*  *Limoux*

Mary Magdalene can usually, but there are a few exceptions, be recognized by the following characteristics.

A beautiful body, sometimes with bare breasts and very long hair, often covering her naked body, but that could also be Mary the Egyptian. Red hair, a sign of royal descent. Her head is most of the time uncovered, while the head of Mother Mary is almost always covered with a veil or crown. Mary Magdalene rarely wears one. Almost always there is a skull at her feet, or in her hands, symbolizing earthly life and its ultimate end, but also reincarnation and wisdom.

Gothic Art

Mirepoix  *Sabart*

Some say that the skull belonged to John the Baptist or even to Jesus. Then an open book, signifying wisdom and her job, as the apostle of apostles, of preaching the teachings of

Jesus. But here she can be confused with Theresa. Often she is holding a small Crucifix in her hand, with Jesus on the cross. Or a bigger wooden cross.

With the book

A cross with leaves, Rennes-le-Chateau

Sometimes the cross has leaves on its stem, signifying living wood, "stating" that Jesus did not die on the cross. A few times I even encountered iron crosses with Mary plus child, and not Jesus, in the center of the cross. Like here in Rennes-les-Bains and in Auriac.

Rennes-les-Bains

Auriac

Then she may be holding a bunch of grapes, stating that she carries the bloodline of Jesus. Or she has a skirt full of roses, showing her fertility. Or holding a palm branch in her hand, referring to her Palestinian descent. Almost always she is depicted with a cup or goblet. Most probably the one used at the last supper, although in the famous wall painting of Leonardo Da Vinci no cup can be seen on the table. Or one or two cruets used to catch the blood and the sweat of Jesus. Or alabaster jars to anoint her lord. Her colors are mostly red

Ax-les-Thermes

Pamiers

and blue or red and green. Sometimes she is dressed in golden garments

She is often compared with the Goddess Venus and thus with the planet Venus. Every 8 years this planet aligns with the sun and earth, resulting, when connected, in a perfect pentagon every 40 years. Sometimes she can be seen with a dove and often her fingers are crossed in a special way. On a few occasions she can be seen holding a red egg, as depicted in chapter 4.

Cave of la Ste. Baume

Abbey of Caunes-Minervoix

At the end of this chapter I will show you some of the most famous faces of Mary Magdalene and some of the most famous scenes. Using only pictures that have not been presented in previous chapters. One should realize however that the way people view Mary Magdalene nowadays can differ considerably from the way people viewed her in the past. How the people saw her in previous centuries depended largely on the way the Church painted her at that time. And with her other women. So please understand that the paintings and statues from past centuries are a reflection of the way she was seen at that time. At the time they were made.

Her face often reflects the following expressions: royal/regal, attractive/sexy, repenting/pensive and sorrow/despair. The most common scenes with Mary Magdalene are: holding a cup or jar, standing at the cross, and being with Jesus when taken off the cross. And I would like to present a few more categories. First the one with "damaged" pictures of Mary Magdalene. They seem to be especially moving, probably because she herself was so often "damaged". And next some special pictures, pictures of Mary Magdalene in strange, unusual situations. Finally one very special category is still missing from this enumeration. That is Mary Magdalene in love. For that important scene I have created a special chapter. See chapter 18.

First let us have a look at her different faces and expressions as I see them:

1. Royal/Regal
2. Attractive/Sexy
3. Repentive/Pensive
4. Sorrow/Despair
5. Holding a cup or jar
6. Standing or sitting at the cross
7. Taken off the cross
8. "Damaged" pictures
9. Noli mi Tangere
10. Boat pictures
11. Pregnant

Royal/regal

In the chapel of the White Penitents in Aigues Mortes and the Notre Dame du Val d'Amour in Belesta. This picture could easily be confused with that of mother Mary, because of the color of her clothes, white and blue. Her loose hair however points to Mary Magdalene.

Notre Dame du Val d'Amour, Belesta

Aigues Mortes

Mary Magdalene in the famous 'Temple' La Madeleine in Paris.

A very self-conscious lady in the Notre Dame de Boulogne-sur-Mer. And an almost arrogant looking Mary Magdalene, taken in a side chapel of the Notre Dame de Grace, high up on the hill behind Honfleur.

Boulogne-sur-Mer

ND du Grâce, Honfleur

And finally Mary Magdalene in St. Martin-Vesubie, in Baune and in Puicheric.

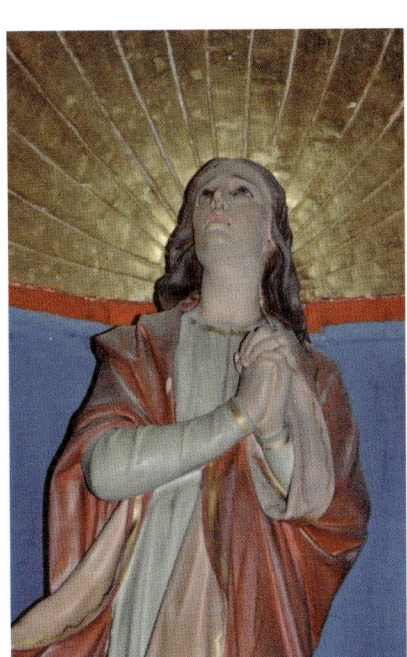

St. Martin-Vesubie

Baune

Puicheric

145

Attractive/sexy

In the basilica of St-Maximin-la-Ste-Baume and in the church of St Paul de Jarrat, between Foix and Tarascon-sur-Ariege.

St. Paul de Jerrat

St. Maximin

And what to think of this lovely woman, coming from the church of Gruissan, a coastal village east of Narbonne.

Gruissan

St. Vincent, Carcassone

And look at the smile on the face of Mary Magdalene in the church of St Vincent in Carcassonne. And in an attractive pose, on the front of the church in Verdelais.

This shield carries all the attributes of Mary Magdalene. It was situated in the sacristy of the Notre Dame du Puy in Le Puy-en-Velay. The people there didn't even realize it was Mary Magdalene. And look at this lovely girl in the Notre Dame de Grace in Honfleur. What a beauty!

Verdelais

Shield, sacristy of le Puy-en-Velay

What a Beauty! Honfleur

And next Mary Magdalene in Corneilla and in a painting of "Annibale Carraci" with in the background the famous Pech Bugarach and in an unknown painting.

Unknown painting

Annibale Carraci

Corneilla-de-Conflent

Church of Ste. Martha, Tarascon-sur-Rhône

And what to think of this woman, lying down very relaxed and showing a beautiful leg in the crypt of the church of Ste. Martha in Tarascon-sur-Rhone. In the same church this stained-glass window can be found. And I adore the small statue, a very old statue, dating from the 14th century. It can be found in the church of St Pierre-Apôtre in St Paul de Fenouillet.

St Pierre-Apôtre in St Paul de Fenouillet 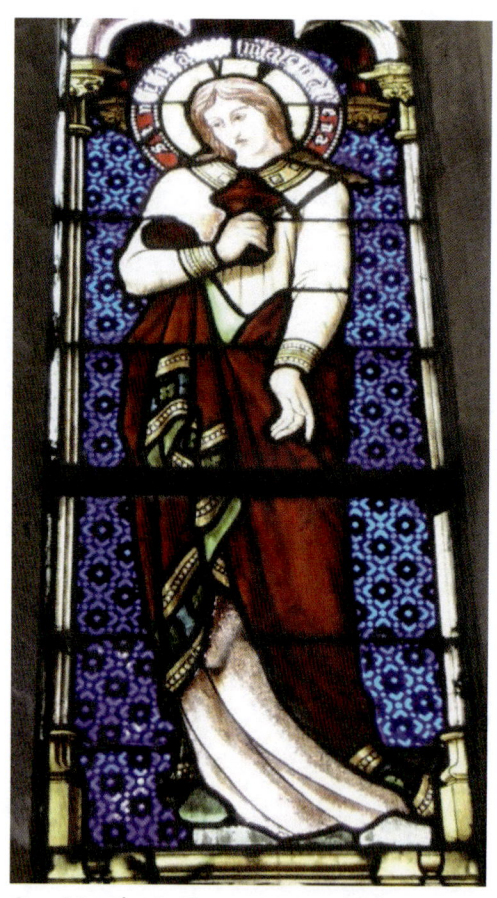   *Ste. Martha in Tarascon-sur-Rhône*

The same applies to this lovely portrait on Limoges porcelain. And the gentle woman in Pomas, and the beautiful woman in Roubia. All beauties.

Church of Pomas

Portrait in Limoges porcelain

Another beauty, Roubia

Repenting/pensive

Let's start with the beautiful wall painting in the Hostellerie La Ste Baume, a place that has been mentioned before. And then go to the abbey of Caunes Minervois, famous for its red marble. Look at the statue of Mary Magdalene. Sad, but resigned and pensive.

Caunes Minervois

Hostellerie La Ste Baume

One of the most moving statues of Mary Magdalene can be found in a cave near Baulou. A special site, where all religious buildings formerly being the Monastery of Carol had to be destroyed, as ordered by the bishop of Pamiers, before this property was sold and handed over to a private person.

Only this statue was spared.

The cave of Baulou, near Foix

Another special picture taken in the Cave of Mary Magdalene in the Ste. Baume Massif, with an etheric cloud just touching her. And these pictures in the church of St. Paul Serge in Narbonne and in the cathedral of Moulins.

Cave of Mary Magdalene in the Ste. Baume

St Paul Serge, Narbonne

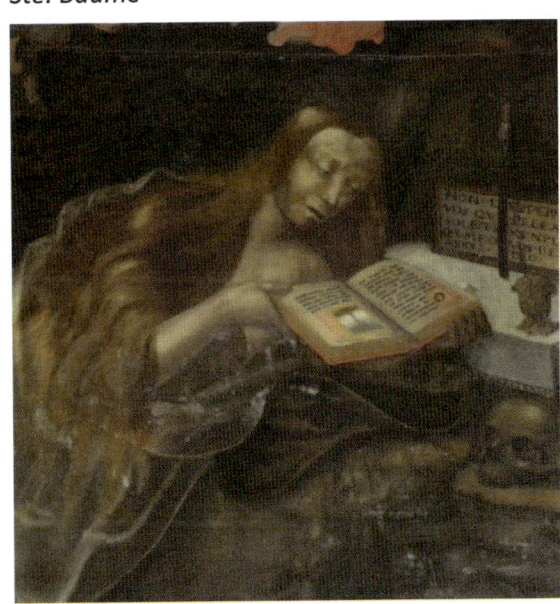

Sacristie of Basilica St Paul Serge, Narbonne

With dove, Moulins

Concluding with two pensive images from the Pyrenees Oriental department.

Corneille-de-Conflent

Ville France-de-Conflent

Sorrow/despair

Many pictures show Mary Magdalene in a state of sorrow and despair. Excluding for the moment the pictures when she is weeping at the foot of the cross. Look at the following pictures. Wonderful topics for gifted artists. In the chapel of Mary Magdalene in the Notre Dame des Pommiers in Belcaire on the Rhone. In the basilica of St-Maximin-la-Ste-Baume, by far the richest ground for pictures and statues of Mary Magdalene. Toulouse also offers quite a lot of pictures of Mary Magdalene. In the Basilica St Sernin and in Le-Puy-en-Velay. And take a look at the heart-rending picture in the magical Notre Dame La Daurade in Toulouse, one of my favorite churches. Just to show how 'rich' Toulouse is in images of Mary Magdalene, see these pictures in the church of St Pierre de Chartreux, also in Toulouse.

Notre Dame des Pommiers in Belcaire

St-Maximin-la-Ste-Baume

Notre Dame de la Daurade

Basilica St Sernin

Le-Puy-en-Velay

St Pierre de Chartreux

One of the most moving faces can be found in the abbey of St Polycarpe, just east of Limoux where Mary Magdalene is both weeping, see the tears, but also radiating. See the aureole around her head.

Abbey of St. Polycarpe

Another picture of a despairing Mary Magdalene can be seen in the basilica of Vezelay, a church that is almost "empty" of pictures and status of Mary Magdalena. Remarkable for Vezelay is the second most important pilgrim site for Mary Magdalena in France. Further pictures full of sorrow and despair can be found in the Notre Dame de Murat, in the church of Vinca, in the Notre Dame de Mende and in the Cathedral of Lavaur.

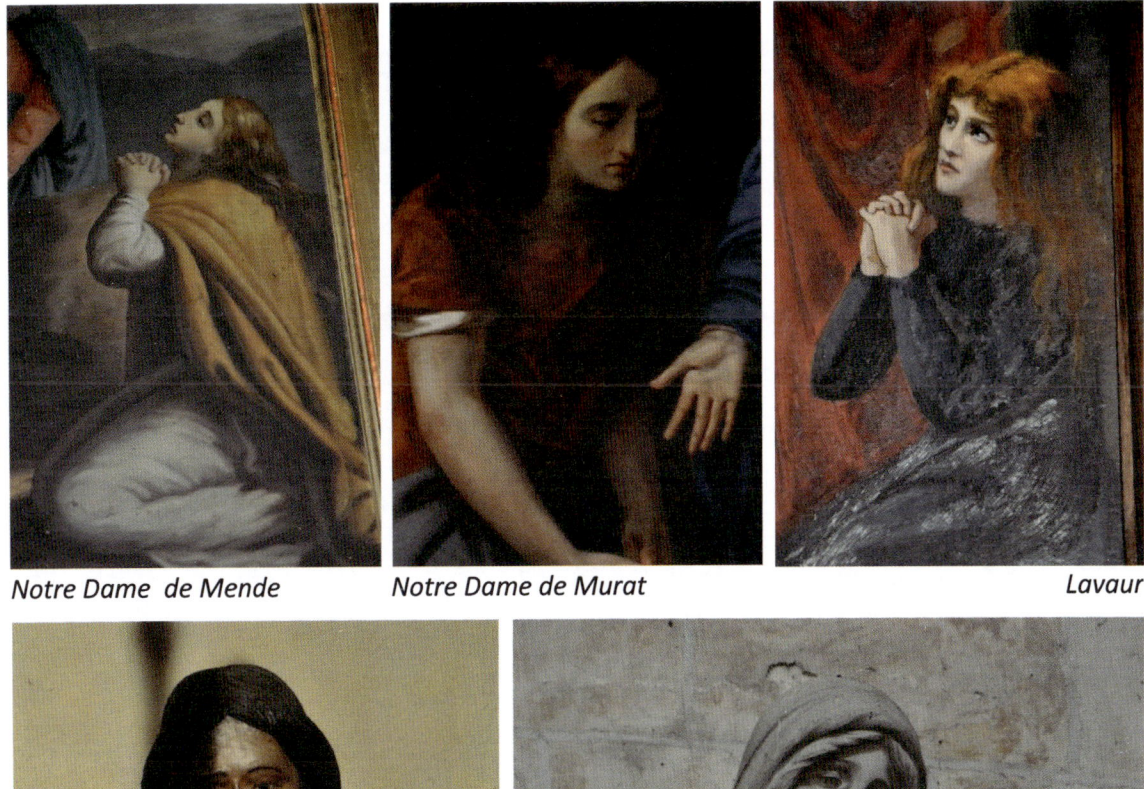

Notre Dame de Mende   *Notre Dame de Murat*   *Lavaur*

Vinca   *Vezelay*

Now we shall continue Mary Magdalene in some of the best known scenes.

155

Holding a cup or jar

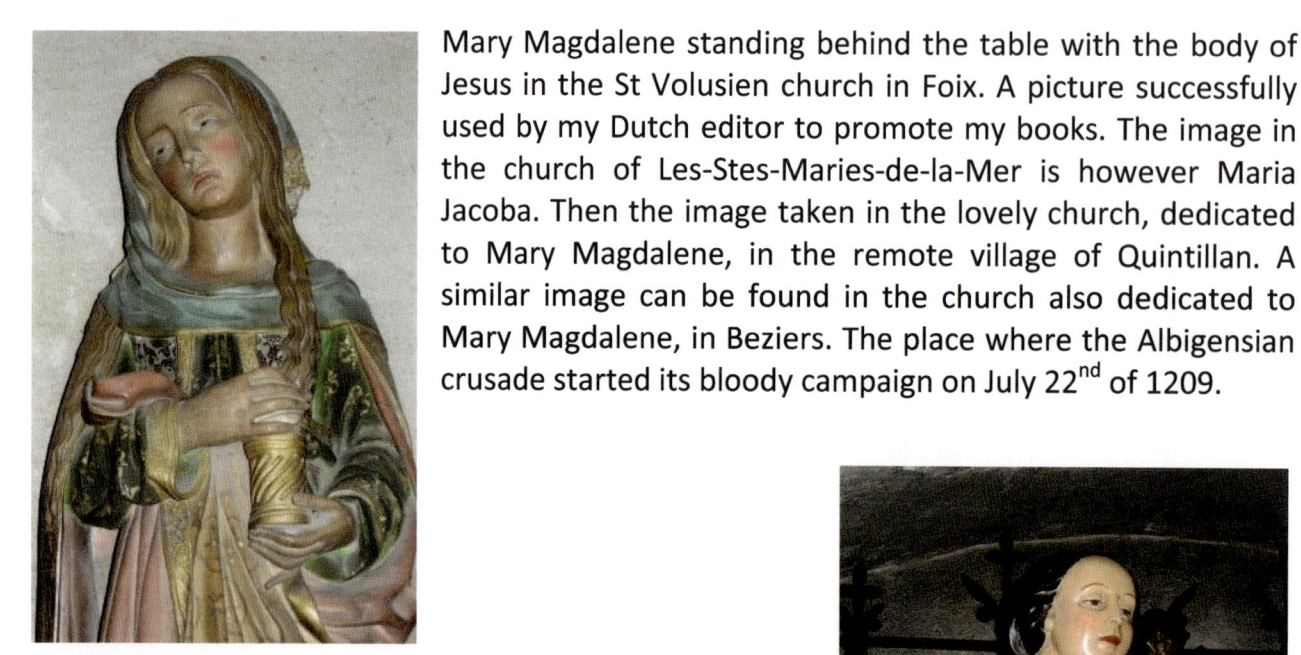

Mary Magdalene standing behind the table with the body of Jesus in the St Volusien church in Foix. A picture successfully used by my Dutch editor to promote my books. The image in the church of Les-Stes-Maries-de-la-Mer is however Maria Jacoba. Then the image taken in the lovely church, dedicated to Mary Magdalene, in the remote village of Quintillan. A similar image can be found in the church also dedicated to Mary Magdalene, in Beziers. The place where the Albigensian crusade started its bloody campaign on July 22nd of 1209.

St. Volusien, Foix

Les-Stes-Maries-de-la-Mer

Quintillan

Béziers

It is interesting to see how different the cups, jars and goblets are. Like in the church of St Martin in Limoux. This could be Mary Magdalene but it could also be one of the three statues symbolizing *La Foie {Belief}, l'Espérance {Hope} and Charité {Love}.* Then of course there is the statue of Mary Magdalene in the church of Rennes-le-Château. And a touching image can also be seen in the Abbey of St Michel de Cuxa, near Prades.

Church of St Martin in Limoux    *Rennes-le-Château*    *Abbey of St Michel de Cuxa*

And what to think of the three Maries in that lovely church of Brenac. The one on the left is Mary Magdalene with cup. And the lovely statue of Mary Magdalene, standing in the crypt of the Basilica St Epvre in Nancy, normally closed for visitors. How sad for it is such a lovely statue.

Brenac

Basilica St Epvre in Nancy

157

More pictures where she is holding a cup or jar can be found in St. Maximin-la-Ste-Baume, in the cathedral of Aix-en-Provence, in Moulins, in Corneilla and in the basilica of Vezelay. But why is she looking so sad, in most of the pictures? Does she know that her love will be crucified soon?

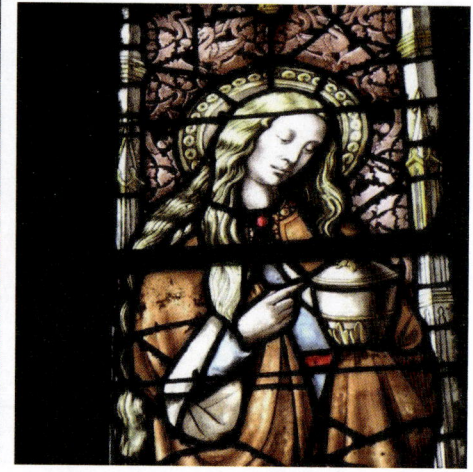

Corneilla

Aix-en-Provence

Aix-en-Provence

Moulins

Vezelay

Standing or sitting at the cross

Most of the pictures at the foot of the cross are very sad. As here in the church of Perillos. A bit confusing now that the apple and the snake have been added. A classic scene, here in the basilica St Sernin in Toulouse. Mother Mary and Mary Magdalene standing beside the cross. With mother Mary *always* on the left. In the crypt of the cathedral of Chartres, in a small room that most people pass by without noticing, on their way to the Notre Dame de Sous-Terre, one of the most outspoken pictures I have ever seen. And this moving picture in the little church of Quintillan, in which Mary tries to soften the pain by embracing Jesus' foot with her hair. And here in the cathedral of Sens.

Church of Perillos

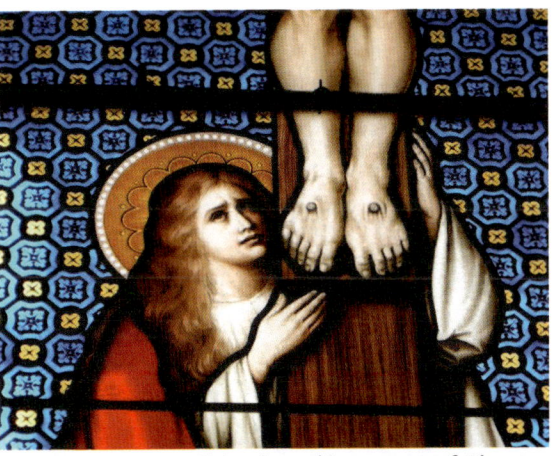

Side chapel in crypte of Chartes

Quintillan

St Sernin, Toulouse

Cathedral of Sens

Next we have a very strange wall painting in the church of St André in Alet-les-Bains where it looks as if a man, a man with an oriental face, carrying a shield with a Chinese dragon, is standing right behind Mary Magdalene. What is he doing there?

St André in Alet-les-Bains

Cathedral Mirepoix

Basilica of St-Maximin-la-Ste-Baume

Then several more pictures, there are hundreds of them in Mirepoix, St-Maximin-la-Ste-Baume, Rennes-le-Château, Nancy, Orval and Peyriac-sur-Mer.

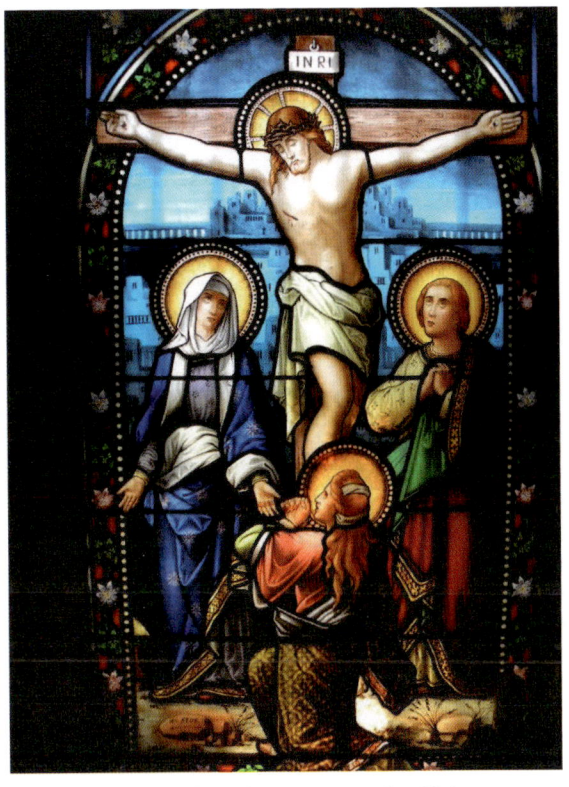

Sacristy of the church in Rennes-le-Château

Notre Dame de Bon Secours in Nancy.

Very old plate at the abbey of Orval

Church of Peyriac-sur-Mer, just south of Narbonne.

And finally, some pictures in a side chapel of the basilica of Vezelay, Troyes, and in the churches of Vinca, Troyes and Bugarach.

Vinca

Side chapel of basilica of Vezelay

Jesus at the cross, Troyes

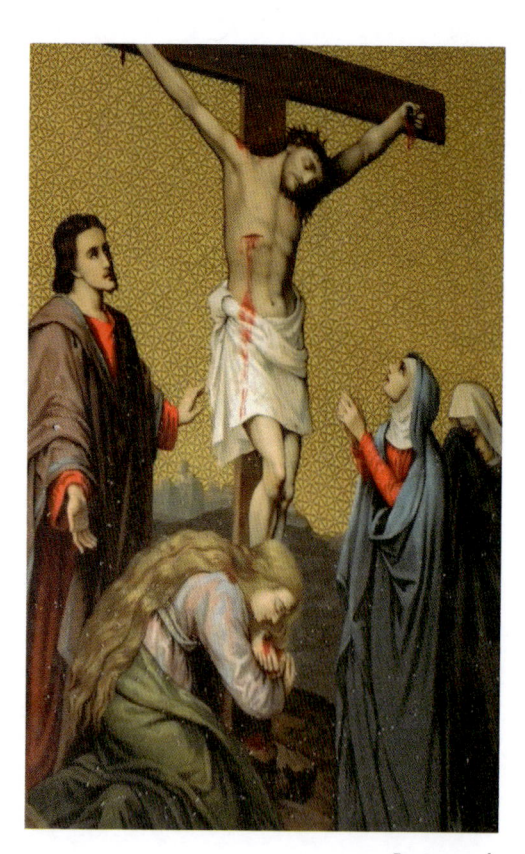

Bugarach

Taken off the cross

These pictures are, if possible, even more moving then the images taken of Mary Magdalene at the foot of the cross. For now her beloved Jesus is dead. All hope is gone. And the process of mourning can start. Look at the mourning woman in the church of Campagne-sur-Aude. Very moving is also the picture taken in the cathedral Notre Dame de Clermont-Ferrand, and in the basilica of St.Maximin-la-Ste-Baume.

Campagne-sur-Aude   *The basilica at St-Maximin-la-Ste-Baume*

Notre Dame de Clermont-Ferrand

Then this vivid, colorful picture of Mary Magdalene kneeling by his site in the Chapelle du Graal in Trehorenteuc, near Broceliande, in the heart of the country of Arthur, Merlin and the Lady of the Lake, right in the middle of Bretagne. The picture clearly shows the customs and culture, the dresses and the faces, of the time it was painted. The same applies for the Notre Dame du Puy.

163

Notre Dame du Puy

Trehorenteuc

Then two beautiful pictures of Mary Magdalene mourning her beloved Jesus. A station of the cross in the Notre Dame de la Fidélité in Douvre la Delivrande. These stations of the cross were painted by a Vietnamese painter and show an uncanny power.

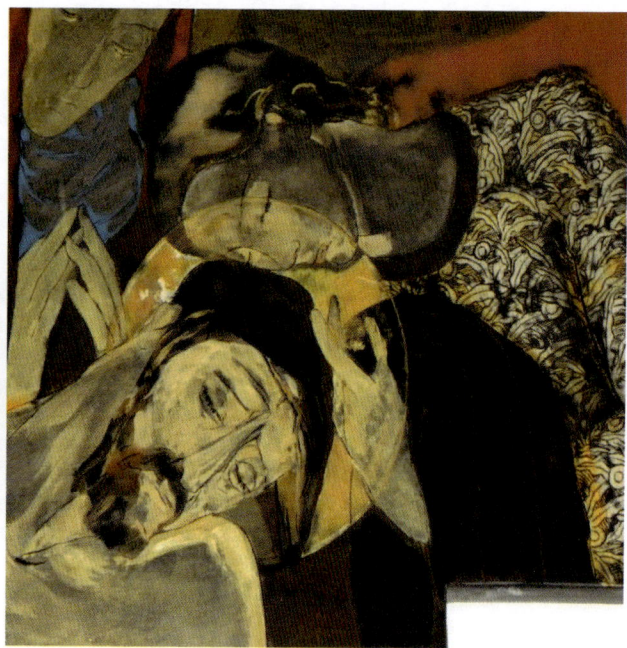

Notre Dame de la Fidélité in Douvre la Delivrande

The same applies for the picture taken in the church of Bram where Mary Magdalene lies with her head on Jesus' knees. And an enlarged look at her sad face.

Bram where Mary Magdalene lies with her head on Jesus' knees.

Finally three more pictures. In the cathedral of Narbonne, Notre Dame du Cros and in the chapel of the Penitents Blancs in Aiges Mortes. Then to conclude this chapter, some "special" pictures.

Chapel des Penitents Blancs, Aigues Mortes

Chapel of Cathedral Narbonne

Notre Dame du Cros

165

"Damaged" pictures

This is a special category, damaged pictures. As mentioned before the churches in France are, since the French Revolution, the responsibility of their communities. But most of the communities have other responsibilities as well and very little money. So the churches and religious artifacts suffer. Even our dearly beloved Mary Magdalene suffers. But, strange as it may be, this seems to make her all the more appealing. Maybe because she herself has been damaged so much. Look at the following pictures, all taken in the basilica of St-Maximin-la-Ste-Baume.

Woodworm

Mary Magdalene as a cupboard cover

Beautiful painting with two huge tears

166

The following pictures show that this does not only happen in St-Maximin-la-Ste-Baume, but also in other places.

Cathedral of St Etienne in Toulouse

Wooden panel in the church of Collioure

Cathedral of Maguelone, south of Montpellier

Cathedral of Narbonne

And in the Chapelle St. Croix in Pomas near Limoux, the cathedral of Rodez, the Eglise Saint-Francois and the church in Montesegur. What a shame, all those beautiful pictures, panels and statues in such a deplorable state. So dear friends when you are in a church with damaged pictures, put some money in the Tronc, or light a candle or do both.

167

Chapelle St Croix, Pomas

Cathedral of Rodez

Church of St. Francois, Lavaux

Church of Montsegur

Noli mi Tangere

Finally there are some other special pictures. Like the "noli me tangere" pictures. The "do not touch me" pictures, or in the right translation, the *"do not cling to me"* pictures.

The basilica of St Maximin

Some pictures have been shown before. But here are more pictures like this. Like in Troyes, in Baune and Mirepoix.

Noli me tangere, Troyes   *Chapel in Beaune*   *Mirepoix*

Boat Pictures

Several boat pictures have been shown in chapter 4. Yet here are some more in Mirepoix and in St-Maximin-la-Ste-Baume. And is not it funny that the Church is still maintaining that Mary Magdalene stayed in Palestine, while so many churches in France show her in a boat on the way to France!

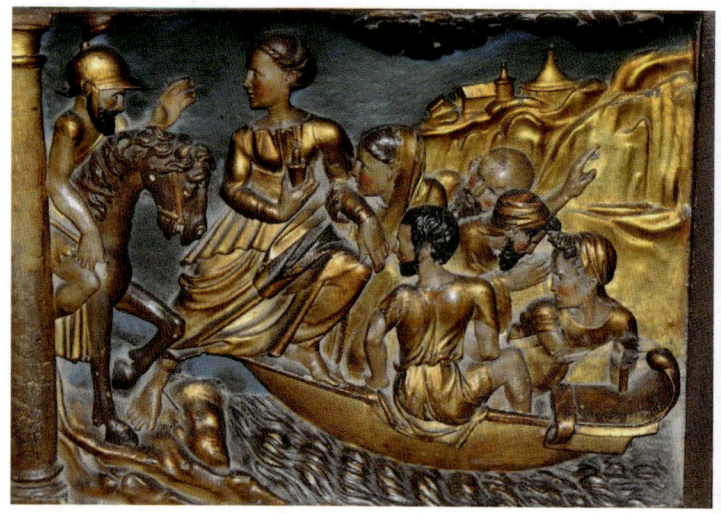

St Maximin

Cathedral of Mirepoix

Exposition in St-Maximin-la-Ste-Baume

Pregnant

Finally statues of a clearly pregnant Mary Magdalene.

Notre Dame du Cros *Abbey of Caunes-Minervois* *Notre Dame de Marceille*

Marie Enciente, Cucugnan

HER LOVE FOR JESUS

There have been and still are fierce discussions as to whether Mary Magdalene was married or not and if she had children or not. The most extraordinary stories have been told. That she had been married before. And that Jesus had been married before. That she was married to John the Baptist. That she was married to a fisherman and left him for Jesus. That she had an affair with Judas. Or that she was not married to Jesus, but was his most beloved companion. Which might explain why the disciples of Jesus asked him why he loved her more then he loved them and why it was specifically mentioned that she often kissed him, presumably on the mouth, as mentioned in the apocryphal gospels. If Jesus was married to Mary Magdalene, such statements might not have been necessary. We just don't know. These are only a few of the stories about Jesus and Mary Magdalene. There are many more. I will stick to the story told by Laurence Gardner, stating that they were married and had three children, Tamar the Sarah, Jesus II and Josephus. And the papyrus document, written in Coptic and recently discovered by Karen King, supports the theory that Jesus and Mary Magdalene were married. See chapter 2.

Fierce discussions are also going on as to whether the person sitting next to Jesus at the Last Supper is John the beloved disciple or Mary Magdalene. Starting with the fresco painted by Leonardo Da Vinci and all the paintings derived from this scene. Discussions started by authors such as Michael Baigent, Lynn Picknett and Clive Prince, Laurence Gardner and Dan Brown. All stating that it is clearly a woman and that this woman can only be Mary Magdalene. A position vehemently opposed by Church and its officials. For them it is a young man, John the beloved disciple. Who often fell asleep with his head on Jesus' shoulders, just because he was so young. A bit farfetched if you ask me. For young people, and certainly people of that age, don't fall asleep. They are just very active.

And if you take a good look at the paintings, fresco's and pictures, it is unmistakably a woman. A woman who is clearly in love with Jesus. However, it is well known that people only see what they expect to see. And if they expect to see John the beloved disciple, then it is John they see. Even if the person has long hair, red lips and a shapely figure. And to make it even more complex there are also researchers who suggest that John the beloved disciple and Mary

Clearly a Woman!

Magdalene are one and the same. And that it was Mary who wrote the Gospel of John. And possibly also a second, secret Gospel.

When you see pictures and panels of the Last Supper, in churches in the "Pays Cathare", there can be little doubt. Little doubt that the mysterious person next to Jesus is a woman. And all these statues and paintings are in plain view, visible in churches and basilicas open to the public, like here in the church of St. Volusien in Foix

But all these discussions about who the person next to Jesus is, seem rather pointless to me. Why is it so important? For nobody is questioning who the person is, appearing in many other, equally important, biblical scenes. Like the anointment of Jesus, like the woman standing at the cross, like the woman consoling Mother Mary, like the "woman with the alabaster jar" to quote the famous book of Margaret Starbird, like the woman mourning the dead Jesus taken from the cross and like the woman meeting him after he has risen from the grave. That woman is clearly Mary Magdalene. No doubt about it. And nobody is questioning that. Then why make such a fuss as to who is sitting next to him at the Last Supper?

St. Volusien in Foix

Then there is the question as to whether Jesus and Mary Magdalene were really in love. Well there are hundreds of pictures, of the Last Supper, the Eucharist ceremony, the marriage of Jesus and Mary Magdalene and many more, showing two people, a man and a woman, unmistakably Jesus and Mary Magdalene, unmistakably in love. Very much in love. No doubt about it.

In Love

Take a look at the following pictures, all from the Cathar country. The images come from various sources. They will not be mentioned here for fear that those places will be visited by too many unwelcome visitors.

174

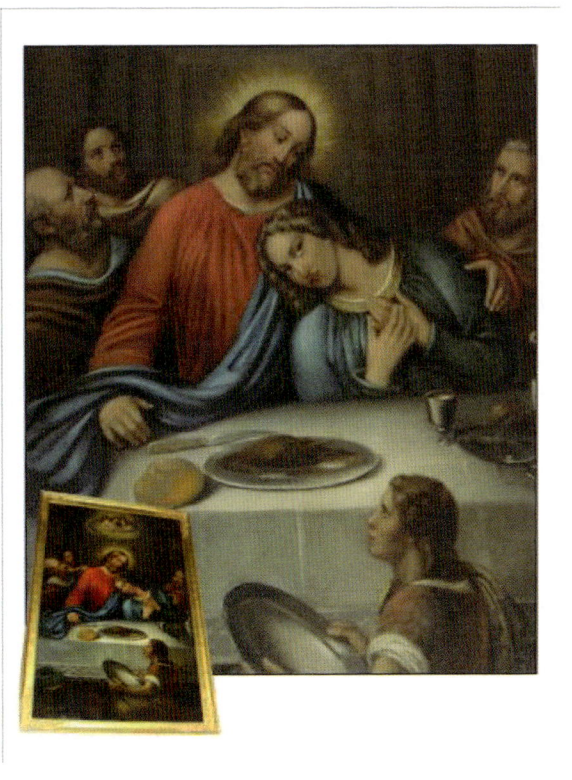

Jesus and Mary Magdalene in Love, Pays Cathare

175

And look at this, a painting made by the well-known Frisian paintress Jeltina Yke Wierda, with the painting on the right as a model. See how much stronger a painting can be than the original!

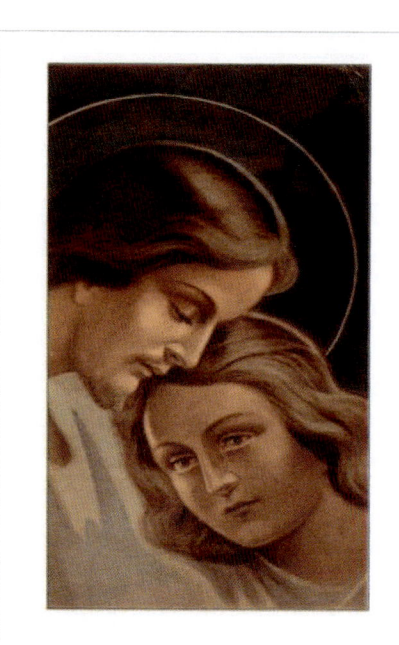

Painting   *Original*

Next there are lots of pictures, big ones and small ones, celebrating the Eucharist, or being baptized, or taking the Holy Communion. Let me share with you some prints in remembrance of the Holy Communion.

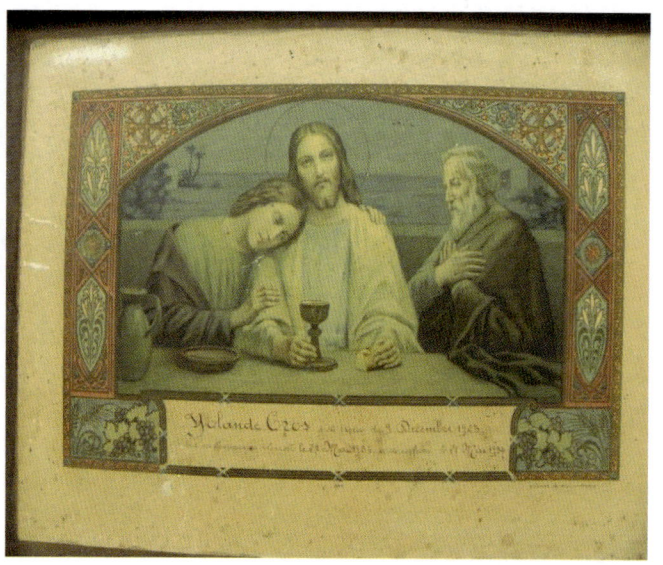

Holy Communion

And presented below many, small pictures where the Eucharist is celebrated. Please note that the women shown in the Eucharist pictures and cards are all older than 11 to 12 years. And all show an uncanny likeness to the Mary Magdalene, leaning lovingly towards Jesus. Well, see for yourself.

Eucharist pictures and cards

Isn't it strange to see that in all these pictures, celebrating the Holy Communion or celebrating the Eucharist, only women can be seen? Not little girls being baptized or girls of about 11 to 12 years old taking the Holy Communion. But women. Young women, grown-up women looking very much like Mary Magdalene. And leaning lovingly against Jesus. I know, the Church will no doubt say that these pictures, statues, paintings, stained-glass windows, panels, cards and many more, are representations of the 'marriage' of young girls to Christ when receiving the Holy Communion. But how about boys being baptized and boys being married to Christ at their first communion? I have not seen any such pictures with boys. And the same applies for the Eucharist ceremony.

Jesus and Mary Magdalene in Love

And in many homes in France you will see these lovely small miniature holy water Fonts. Made of wood or marble, with Jesus and Mary Magdalen close together.

178

SACRED FEMININITY

Our western societies have, in the past 2,000 years, become male dominated societies. Driven by power and greed. Striving for material wealth, personal gain and getting results, whatever the costs. Controlled by fear, sin and guilt. With little regard for the lives and the welfare of other people. And no tolerance for dissentient views. And how we suffered for that. With endless wars, severe prosecutions, violent crusades, religious wars, revolutions, genocides, battles where thousands of innocent people were killed. Speaking for France alone, think of the brutal Crusades to the Holy Land. Think of the Albigensian crusade were over 300,000 fellow Christians, the Cathars, were killed or burned alive. Think of the apprehension of the Knights Templar. And the disastrous activities of the inquisition, followed by terrible witch-hunts. Think of the terrible religious wars. Think of the continuous fighting at almost every corner of the land. Think of the many wars that ravished their colonies. Followed by the bloody French Revolution.

Peace be with You

Finally resulting in the most violent age in recorded history, the twentieth century. Where worldwide more than 200 million people lost their lives in wars, uprisings and freedom fights. Where religion was often the issue, but where power and material wealth were the real motives. When will we ever learn?

Hopefully now, now that Mary Magdalene is making her way back. After almost 2,000 years. Back in our minds. Back in our hearts. "Rising", so to speak, from where it all began, from France, the second Holy Land. The land where she preached so lovingly and so forcefully. The land of the powerful Visigoths, the mysterious Merovingian's and the mighty Carolingians. The Land of the Cathars with their pure, "Gnostic" beliefs.

The land where most of the Knights Templar could be found. The knights who had sworn allegiance to The House of Bethany and who fiercely protected her legacy. The Templars who built the beautiful cathedrals, basilicas and churches, dedicated to Mary Magdalene. The land where powerful kings and cardinals ruled, right up to the French Revolution. And where after the French Revolution, an even more powerful man arose, Napoleon Bonaparte. The man who went to Rome when the Pope excommunicated him. A land with eminent scientists, willful bishops and learned religious study groups, for example at the St. Sulpice in Paris. With famous priests in the area of Rennes-le-Château, like Bigou, Boudet, Gelis and Saunière. With many, powerful, secret societies and their dark secrets.

Cathedral of Chartres

With Otto Rahn and the German SS searching the Pays Cathare during the Second World War.

Yes, it all happened in France, especially in the Languedoc area.

St. Sulpice, Paris

After the war we saw a revival of Catharism. The story of the million-dollar priest Saunière came out and Mary Magdalene 'resurfaced'. Important discoveries were made in the Middle East. The search for the historical Jesus and Mary Magdalene had begun. The discovery of the Nag Hammadi parchments in 1945 in Egypt brought many lost gospels to light. And the Dead Sea Scrolls discovered in 1947 in Qumran, shed a different light on the events during the times of Christ. And recently in 2000, the Gospel of Judas was found. And in 2012 a papyrus document was discovered where Jesus speaks of this wife.

Shocking facts are now surfacing about the wheeling and dealings of the Church in the past millennia. About their manipulations, their falsifications, their power plays and hypocrisy. Bestsellers like "*The Holy Blood and the Holy Grail*" and the "*Da Vinci Code*" opened our eyes to the tricks of the Church. And our hearts to Mary Magdalene. She was reborn. Supported by many more discoveries of ancient documents in universities, abbeys and private collections. People got further inspired by the huge amount of channeled information and the many visions that became available. Information about the historical Jesus and Mary Magdalene. Published in wonderful books. People became interested in other, oriental religions, like Buddhism and Hinduism. Religions that take a different view on this life and the lives hereafter. It is a wonderful time. A time of awakening. Admirers of Mary Magdalene are touched by the many portraits, paintings and statues, published in books and catalogues. We are witnessing an awakening of spirituality. And a revival of sacred femininity. Fuelled by powerful emancipation movements, where women are, at least in the western world, equal to men. If not more so. "Thank Heaven", or should I say "Thank God" for Mary Magdalene. She is back. Back in our life, back in our hearts. But she was never far away. Only we, the common people, we didn't know. She was always there, in France, especially in de south of France, remembered and revered by millions of people. She was held in high regard by royalty and nobility, who saw her as the "Daughter" or the "Mother" of France. And who were proud of their descent from Jesus and Mary Magdalene.

She was also known to monks and nuns, living in abbeys and cloisters, who could read books and religious documents not available to the general public. They too had a high regard for her. She was present in the Languedoc, but sub surface. Far away from Rome and far away from Paris. She was known to educated people, people who could read and write. Who studied the bible. Knowledgeable people, scientists, both inside and outside the church. They too held her in high regard. And she was known to the members of secret societies. Societies that possessed throughout the ages volatile secrets and forbidden documents relating to Mary Magdalene. So she was not completely unknown. But now, in the 21st century, now the situation is different. Now she is known to practically everyone in the Western world. They have all heard of her. And with the emancipation well under way and the "awakening" of Mary Magdalene almost complete, "sacred femininity" has entered our world. About time, I would say. For we have suppressed the female principle far too long. And we had to go without the moderating influence of women far too long. We lost the healthy, creative power of women. We became immune for the creative and destructive powers of ancient Goddesses, like Kali and Sarah in Les-Stes-Maries-de-la-Mer.

Kali in Les-Stes-Maries-de-la-Mer

Sarah in Les-Stes-Maries-de-la-Mer

There was not much compassion, little wisdom, and almost no love in our lives. Especially love. Love for ourselves, for our friends and family, for mankind, for nature and for the earth. Universal love.

We didn't realize that men and women have male and female energies. And that those energies must be balanced. Otherwise we live unbalanced lives. Unsatisfactory lives, lives full of stress, frustration and burn-out. We forgot to use our common sense. And let ourselves be manipulated by governments and churches that were preaching fear, anger, eternal guilt and damnation. We lost the ability to see with our hearts. We wanted to be pampered and amused, from our birth to our death. Far too many people live passive lives. They are not interested in what happens in the world, in what happens to Mother Earth. They don't care for other people, but watch television, play computer games, eat and drink and go to amusement parks. Or bingo's! What a life!

But now sacred femininity is back. The power of women is growing. More men respect their women. And some even fear them. Spirituality is growing. Ancient wisdom is surfacing. Universal love is entering our hearts and our minds. More and more men are honoring their women, as we did in the 11th and 12th centuries. The time of courtly love. More and more men see their women as magical creatures, as Goddesses. Possessing incredible powers. The power of love. The power to make us into real men. Women can make men happy, with their love and their laughter. Or sad, with their anger and scorn. They are the Goddesses who make sex a wonderful experience. Who transform it from lust to love. They are so beautiful. Let them blossom, let them be free. And let us men cherish them with our love and attention. Realizing that they are no longer our possession, but free spirits.

St. Paul de Fenouillet

Women are born to live, to laugh, to love and to create.

There is so much love in the Languedoc that it even shows in the landscape. See the beautiful heart in the Fontaine des Amours near Rennes-les-Bains.

Fontaine des Amours near Rennes-les-Bains.

Or the wonderful heart cut out by the river Agly in the famous Gorges de Galamus. The spectacular canyon running from Cubières to St. Paul-de-Fenouillet. Where a road was cut out in the rocks during the 19th century and where an ancient monastery exists with a church inside the rock.

River Agly

Look at the land south of Rennes-le-Château. And at the heart in the tree, in the river and in the snow. All hearts, all Love.

In the valley of Rennes-le-Chateau

In the river

In a tree

In the air

Cité, Carcassonne

There is even love in the basilica of the Cité in Carcassonne. Love between mother and child. A picture showing a bare breast! A picture that, if the breast had been "alive", and had been seen on TV, might throw half the population of the USA in turmoil!

There are many books written about sacred femininity. For example the book "*The Magdalene Awakening, Symbols & Synchronicity Heralding the Re-emergence of the Divine Feminine*" by L. Shannon Andersen.

But many women are still angry with men. Women who suffer or suffered from male domination. Or who suffer on behalf of all the women who suffered in the past. Some of them took their anger out on me. For I am a man. And I represent in their eyes, all the evil done by men in the past. I can understand that these women are angry, but this is not the way. For that happened in the past. To illustrate my point I tell them that in one of my previous lives I was a woman, living in Paris during the French Revolution. Where I was betrayed by a man, molested, tortured, raped and finally send to the guillotine. Then I tell her that it could have been her who betrayed me. That she could have been that horrible man in Paris, in her past life.

And finally a wonderful picture, symbolizing the power and love of the Sacred Femininity. See this beautiful friend of mine, so lovely and so powerful, standing in front of Pech Cardou, the female mountain, near Rennes-le-Château.

Sacred Feminity

And this woman, portrayed in the alley leading to the Goddess Temple in Glastonbury. The City of Sacred Feminity.

THE SECOND HOLY COUNTRY

France can rightfully be called "The Second Holy Country". Even if she did not always act like a Holy Country. But that was not so different in the first Holy Country. Why should France be called the Second Holy Country? Well, you could say that it is her heritage. Her Christian heritage. The heritage of Jesus and Mary Magdalene. The heritage of powerful Roman emperors. The heritage of the Cathars and the Knights Templar. The heritage of her kings and emperors. The heritage of her bishops and cardinals. And the heritage of the common people. France is the rightful heir of Christianity. And not only her heir, but also the protector of the "State Christianity" of the Church and "Gnostic Christianity" of the Cathars. France as the powerbase of Christianity. The land where kings and cardinals ruled the land, right up to the French Revolution.

It is the place where Mary Magdalene went when she fled from Palestine. It doesn't matter where she landed, she landed in France. She lived here, she preached here, she baptized here. She, and probably Jesus as well, are most likely buried in France. Again, it does not matter where, it is in France. What matters is that she is lovingly remembered in France. That she lives in the hearts of the people. She is everywhere. In basilicas, churches, chapels, books, writings, and paintings. She can be heard in myths, legends and folktales. She is "alive". Her presence "radiates" in the churches and chapels dedicated to her. Her face can be seen everywhere. In the Stations of the Cross. In the hundreds of statues and paintings in churches and basilicas and in the thousands of Holy Communion and Eucharist cards in the homes of the people.

Mary Magdalene in Pamiers

France is the place where Christianity, true Christianity, first set foot on land. I know that Paul brought Christianity to Turkey, Greece and Italy, but I am not sure that his teachings were those of Jesus and Mary Magdalene. Most probably they were his own, "Romanized" versions of Christianity, infused with elements of other, then popular religions. In France true Christianity arrived with Mary Magdalene.

And took hold. It wasn't called France at that time but Gaul, the land of the Celts, the land conquered by Julius Caesar. How wonderful that near Gergovia, the place where Vercingetorix was beaten, now stands, in Le-Puy-en-Velay, the huge iron statue of the Notre Dame de France.

Of course, Christianity also survived elsewhere, in the First Holy Country, in Israel or Palestine, with the Nazarenes. It came to the British Isles with Joseph of Arimathea, where it blended nicely with the Celtic beliefs and the Druid cultures to evolve into the Celtic church. The Church that later, during the Dark Middle Ages, revived the fading Christian faith in the rest of Europe. On the Continent, as the British would say. It survived in Egypt with the Copts and in Eastern Europe as the Greek and Russian Orthodox religions. It flourished for a while in Armenia and in Iraq and maybe even in Tibet. And many other places. But it was nowhere so strong, so pure and so deeply embedded in the land and in the hearts of the people, as in France.

Notre Dame de France

To France I would like to say: "France, please wake up. You are the second Holy Country. You have a responsibility. Take that responsibility. The Church is fast losing ground. Help the Church to turn the tide. Help the people all over the world to keep their faith. You as the guardian of Mary Magdalene's legacy, you can do it."

I would even be so bold as to say: "Use Mary Magdalene, use her heritage, use her charisma, use her love. Use it to help the church survive. Not the Church, meaning the Vatican, the Pope, the cardinals or the bishops. They are beyond help. But the church, the church of the common people. The church of the many priests, nuns and other Christian workers, who are helping people all over the world. Helping the poor, setting up schools and hospitals. The people who are doing the work started by Jesus and Mary Magdalene. These men and women should be recognized, honored and protected. Don't let them go down with the Vatican. The true Christians, the people in the field; they need your support, your backing, your money. Don't let them down!"

And I am not only talking about the Roman Catholic Church, but about all Christian churches. The workers of these churches need a solid base. It doesn't matter if they are Catholic or Protestant. Besides both religions were known in France. Now is not the time to highlight the differences between the churches. That has been done long enough and with terrible results. Now it's time to work together. To create a common base. A base to help the true workers to continue their work.

And France, beautiful France, if you are still not fully convinced of your "status" as Second Holy Country, let me remind you of who you are and what you have. Let me show you your Christian heritage and your Christian assets.

France has always had a special connection with Palestine. Especially the Provence and Languedoc regions and later the Auvergne, Bourgogne, Aquitane and Lorraine. It could have been the land where the lost Tribe of Benjamin took refuge. Many hundreds of years BC. The area around Rennes-le-Château has for ages been a Sacred Area, so they must have known about it. It is a land with two Holy Mountains, the Pech Bugarach and the Pech Cardou. Or even three Holy mountains, including the 2,785 meter high Pic du Canigou in the French Pyrenees..

The two Sacred Mountains

Pech Bugarach

Pech Cardou

Mountains often compared with Mount Sinai in the Sinai desert and the Temple Mount in Jerusalem. Then there is the story that the Jews, in the 6th century BC, built a temple of Solomon under the Pech Cardou. A temple where the Arc of the Covenant could have been placed. We often see pictures of the Ark in churches in this area. Like in the Notre Dame de Marceille in Limoux, the Notre Dame du Val d'Amour in Belesta and the cathedral of Chartres. This land was both sacred and far away from Palestine and Jerusalem when

St. Vincent, Carcassougne *Alet-les-Bains*

Nebuchadnezzar conquered the city in 586 BC and destroyed the Temple. Later many Jewish families lived in this area. Either because they were rich or because they had been banished from Palestine. And Jewish families still live here. Several synagogues can be found in the area. Several churches have the Star of David in their windows, like here in Carcassonne and in Alet-les-Bains and Beaucaire.

Mary Magdalene, most likely with her beloved Jesus, came to France. Where she preached the teachings of Jesus. Where she founded Christianity, true Christianity. Mary Magdalene who has been called both the "Mother of France" and the "Daughter of France". Mary Magdalene who was preaching Love, spiritual growth and compassion. Teachings that went straight to the hearts of the people. Teachings that were gladly absorbed by the land.

Jesus and Mary Magdalene founded the royal houses of France. Such as the Merovingian's, the counts of Toulouse, Aquitaine, Bourgogne and Lorraine. The houses of Acqs and the Fisher kings. They are probably buried in France. Some of their bones and their skulls might be entombed in various churches and basilica's in the country. France always had powerful Kings who saved the Church for France or France for the Church, depending on what view you take. Like King Clovis who was baptized in 496 in Reims. And Charles Martel who stopped the Saracens at Poitiers in 732 AD. Or Charlemagne who firmly consolidated his vast empire.

Or Louis the Saint who went twice on a crusade to the Holy Land. And who is revered as a saint in many churches in France.

Charlemagne

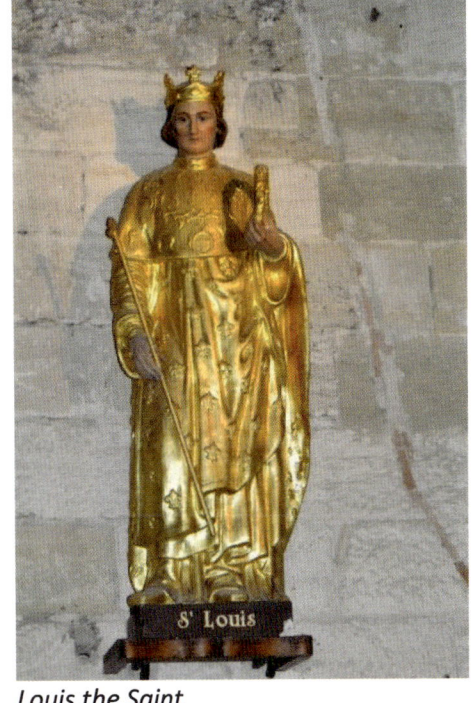

Louis the Saint

Or Louis XIV, "Le Roi Soleil" who drove the English, the Spanish and the Germans out of what is now France. And the Languedoc was where Catharism sprang up. Growing from the seeds sown by Jesus and Mary Magdalene. It was the land where the Knights Templar were most powerful.

Louis XIV, "Le Roi Soleil"

Finally no other country in the world has so many churches dedicated to Mary Magdalene. And so many Black Virgins or Black Madonna's. See chapter 16. Nowhere in the world will you find so many chapels, churches, basilicas and cathedrals with statues, paintings and stained glass windows of Mary Magdalene. And nowhere else will you find so many statues of Anne the grandmother of Jesus with her daughter Mary. And sometimes together with Mary and the infant Jesus on her arm, as a new kind of Holy

Anna and Mary, Canet d'Aude

Anna, Mary and Jesus in Paimpont

And in Notre Dame de Grace, Honfleur

Trinity.

Nowhere else you will find so many Holy Communion cards, so many baptism cards and so many Eucharist cards were Jesus and Mary Magdalene are portrayed close together. And nowhere else, as far as I know, you will see scenes of their marriage or scenes where Jesus and Mary Magdalene sit together, at equal height, let alone scenes where they lean towards each other as lovers. And nowhere else will you see pregnant Maries.

No fewer than 4 official pilgrim routes lead from Sacred Places in France to St Jacques de Compostelle in Spain. Being the Chemin de Tours, starting from Chantilly and Paris and passing Chartres or Orleans, Tours, Poitiers, Aulnay and Bordeaux. The others being The Chemin de Vezelay, passing through Limoges, Perigueux and the Chemin du Puy, starting in Le-Puy-en-Velay and passing through Villefrance-de-Rouerge and Cahors or Rocamadour and Agen.

Lovers

The fourth being the Chemin du Piémont Pyrénéen, starting in Arles and passing through St Gilles, Montpellier, St-Guilhem-le-Desert, Toulouse and Auch, or Narbonne, Carcassonne, Pamiers and St-Bertrand-de-Comminges. All coming together at St-Jean-Pied-de-Port, near Roncevaux or Oloron-Ste-Marie, before crossing over to Spain.

Yes, France can truly be called the Second Holy Country!

A PILGRIMAGE

Come to France. It is a beautiful country. The country where the roots of Christianity are deeply embedded in the land. In the churches and basilicas, in the castles, in the stones, in the land itself and in the hearts of the people. And contrary to what many people may think, French people are very nice. Gentle, hospitable, polite. Only in the big cities people are a bit more stressed, but that is the same in all big cities in the world.

Visit France, the second Holy Country. Visit the places of beauty. Visit the places where Mary Magdalene is revered. Where you can still feel her energy. Visit the sacred places of the Black Madonna's. And feel their creative energy and their love.

There are many places worth visiting for those who want to follow in the footsteps of Mary Magdalene. All her sacred sites, all her caves, all her basilicas, churches and chapels, all the places where she is honored. Where beautiful paintings are, magnificent statues, pilgrimages, festivities and celebrations. I will mention only the most interesting places. Many places have already been discussed in previous chapters, so I will only mention them and not elaborate.

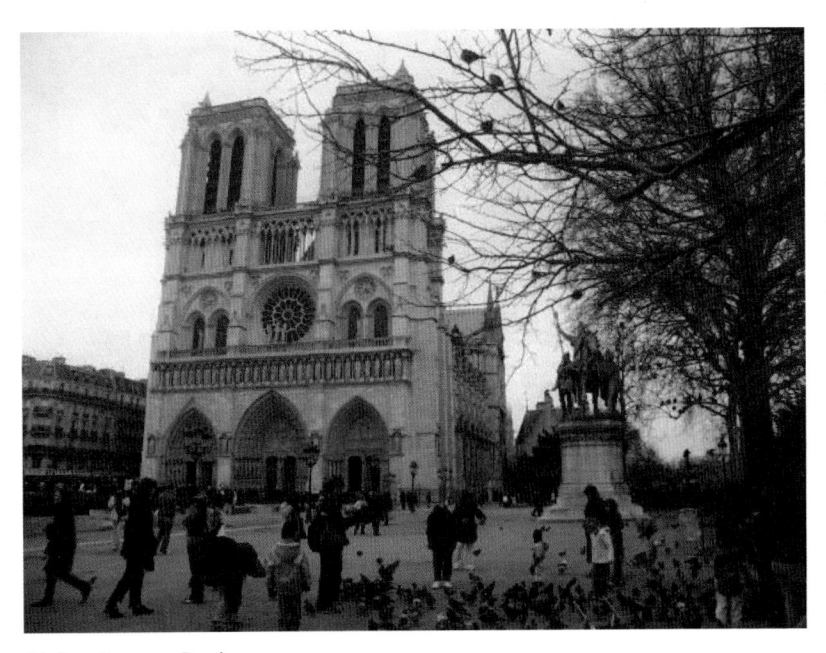

Notre Dame, Paris

Of course one should start in Paris. Visit the cathedral Notre Dame on the Ile de la Cité and the Sainte Chapelle, on the same isle, with its magnificent, brilliant stained glass windows. Visit the magic St. Sulpice basilica, well known from the *"Da Vinci Code"*.

And of course the imposing church La Madeleine, built after the French Revolution. And maybe one of the 16 churches, chapels and museums in and around Paris where statues of the Black Madonna can be found. Don't forget the famous Sacré Coeur, built at the end of the 19th century and financed, some say, by the treasures found in Rennes-le-Château. Then on to Troyes, in my view the city where, at the court of the Dukes of Bourgogne, information surfaced that led to the first crusade and to the establishment of the Order of the Knights Templar.

The oldest church in the city is dedicated to Mary Magdalene, a beautiful church.

From Troyes we go to Metz. With the Notre Dame de la Rotonde, now part of the cathedral of St Etienne and the Black Madonna Notre Dame de Bon-Secours. Located on the place where once a temple of Diana stood.

La Madeleine, Paris

Church in Troyes

Cathedral in Metz

Notre Dame de Bon Secours

Going south to Nancy, capital of Lorraine. The city with her many, beautiful buildings, her imposing cathedral, the Notre Dame de Bon Secours and another favorite, the basilica of St Epvre. A little further South is Sion-Vaudemont, with the Notre Dame de Sion on the "Colline Inspire", the Inspired Hill. Further south to Dijon and her beautiful Notre Dame the Dijon, holding the mysterious Black Madonna Notre Dame de Bon-Espoir, who performed many miracles.

Basilica of St Epvre

Notre Dame of Dijon

Here we make a small step west, to Vezelay. The city full of controversy over who has the true real relics of Mary Magdalene. Don't get mixed up in that argument, but admire the incredible beauty of the church, the tympanum with its many statues and its beautiful sacred geometry and the crypt where, so they say, one of her bones is kept.

Porch of Vezelay

Notre Dame de Sion in Sion-Vaudemont

And look at the majestic the inside of the basilica of Vazelay. Really awesome.

Basilica Vezelay

But most of all admire the location of the church. It is pure magic on top of that hill. And, if you want to buy books about Mary Magdalene, this is the place. I have never seen a place where so many spiritual books and more specifically books about Mary Magdalene are for sale. With maybe one exception, Glastonbury in England.

Then to Baune, a beautiful city in the middle of the Bourgogne with her characteristic Notre Dame.

Notre Dame of Baune

Then onward to Lyon, to the magnificent basilica Notre Dame de Fourviere on top of the hill. The old city on top of the hill is now a Unesco World Heritage site.

Next to the basilica is the chapel of St Thomas a Becket, housing two Black Madonna's.

Then a little to the south and west, crossing the river Rhone, to a place called Le Pilat. The place where the count of Roussillon reigned and where his widow built a church dedicated to his memory. With a lovely statue in the porch of the church and a wonderful drawing of Mary Magdalene with child. Looking very much like Mary Magdalene in the church of Rennes-le-Château.

Notre Dame de Fourviere

Le Pilat

Mary Magdalene in le Pilat

Before going to the Provence we turn east at Valence and go up into the Alps to a place called Ay, near Chambery with its magic church and the Black Madonna of Myans.

The next stop is the Provence. A region full of Mary Magdalene. A region of majestic mountains, beautiful trees and the dark blue Mediterranean Sea. There is so much to be seen and so much to enjoy in this area. The mountains, the sea, the churches, the people, the colors, the food. You might go to Avignon first where for a time the French popes ruled. Then to Arles, the city of van Gogh, known for its cult of Isis and Cybele.

With the church dedicated to St. Trophimus. From there to Aix-en-Provence where Maximus and Sidonius went after arriving in France with Mary Magdalene. To the basilica of Ste. Marie Madeleine, located on the spot where Mary Magdalene might have been buried. Yes, Mary Magdalene is very much present in Aix-en-Provence. Look at these beautiful pictures of her in the cathedral of Saint-Sauveur. Which in itself is unusual. As there are rarely pictures of Mary Magdalene in a cathedral.

St. Trophimus, Arles

Cathedral of Saint-Sauveur

And 40 km's east of Aix is the famous basilica St-Maximin-la-Sainte-Baume and its rich interior and its many paintings and statues of Mary Magdalene. A place that has been discussed at length before.

Basilica St-Maximin-la-Sainte-Baume

Then South to Plan-d'Aups to the Hostellerie, with her beautiful chapel. An up to the cave of Sainte Baume, by the "road of the kings" to the Cave of Mary Magdalene. With her impressive statues, stained glass windows and marvelous view.

Before heading West we might make a trip to the East to Cannes and Nice and then North, up into the Alps-Maritimes. To Saint-Martin Vesubie with its sanctuary, 1900 meters high, of the Notre Dame de Fenetre. Then back again and westwards along the coast to the old city of Marseille.

Inside the cave in La Ste. Baume

Where on the east side of the old harbor stands the church of St Victor. In the old crypt, dating back to the first Christian cemetery in the 4th century AD, you will find a relief of Mary Magdalene with skull and a portrait of Lazarus. And it is certainly worthwhile to go a little further up the hill to the famous basilica, the Notre Dame de la Garde, with its beautiful black Madonna, its many paintings of ships and the huge, golden statue of the Virgin on top of the church.

Lazarus in the crypte of St. Victor, Marseille

Then to the Languedoc, the region west of the Rhone River, stretching all the way to the Pyrenees and Toulouse. First we will visit the church of Les-Saintes-Maries-de-la-Mer where the three Maries came on land. If possible on the 24th of May, the day of Sarah, or the 25th of May, the day of Mary Salome.

Les-Saintes-Maries-de-la-Mer

We follow the coast, the beautiful wild delta of the Camarque to Aigues Mortes. A fortified city on the coast. With many statues of Louis the Saint and some of Mary Magdalene. One with red hair and one clearly pregnant. Following the coast further to the west we will pass the strange cathedral of Maguelone, the fishing village Sète, the old Greek colony of Agde to arrive at the beautiful port of Gruissan just east of Narbonne, with this lovely picture in the church. Could that be Mary Magdalene?

Mary Magdalene? in Gruissan

More inland is another route touching several interesting places. Like the city of Tarasçon-sur-Rhône with its church dedicated to Martha. Where she beat a dragon by holding a cross in front of its eyes. Across the river is Baucaire with a special chapel dedicated to Mary Magdalene. A little further west is St Gilles, with its wonderful ancient abbey and its huge crypt.

Church of Ste. Martha

Abbey of St. Gilles

Going further West we arrive at Béziers, the place where the Albigensian crusade started its brutal march. With an imposing church dedicated to Mary Magdalene. Very impressive, especially when remembering that hundreds of people were burned alive at that place on July 22nd of the year 1209.

To arrive finally in Narbonne, the old Roman capital of Gaul. In the cathedral Saint-Just-et-Saint-Pasteur you will see several images of Mary Magdalene. Strange, but the more damaged her paintings and statues are, the more they seem to "touch" our hearts.

Béziers

Then we could make a small detour to the south. To Fitou, Port La Nouvelle and to Ste-Marie-la-Mer, just north of Perpignan, with another lovely statue of Mary Magdalene in the church of Ste-Marie-la-Mer. Another place where Mary Magdalene could have landed when she came to France. South of Perpignan is the wonderful, tourist port of Collioure. Where the Knights Templar had a castle and a large commandery. The little church at the harbor entrance is certainly worth a visit. A highly decorated and beautiful church with several wonderful paintings of Mary Magdalene.

Collioure

Then over to the Cathar country. A lot has been said about Rennes-le-Château, but there are many other places worth visiting. Like St Paul de Fenouillet, with the old 14th century statue of Mary Magdalene. And Cucugnan with its pregnant Mary. Or the Notre Dame de Laval with its beautiful statue of Mary with child. Further South, in the Pyrenees, are many beautiful places to visit. Like Thuir, Vinca, the abbey of St. Michel in Prades and the abbey of St. Martin de Canigou, high up in the mountains. Furthermore the magic churches of Corneille de Conflent and Ville France de Conflent. And if you are up to it, near the Spanish border, the church in Prats-de-Mallo. Then further North to Alet-les-Bains. A very old city with the most beautiful abbey ruin in France. The abbey was destroyed during the religious wars. Well worth a visit is also the church of St André, with its four stained glass windows with the Star of David. And the curious fresco depicting Jesus on the cross with the Virgin Mary and Mary Magdalene on each side, while behind the two Maries strange persons, with oriental faces can be seen.

And most certainly Limoux with the church of St Martin, portraying, for everyone to see, the marriage of Jesus and Mary Magdalene. And another window showing Mary sitting at equal height with Jesus.

A few miles north of Limoux is the famous Notre Dame de Marceille, with its new Black Madonna. The previous one has been stolen. There are some powerful abbeys in the area. In Lagrasse, Fontfroide, St Hilaire and Polycarpe. The last one with a very impressive face of Mary Magdalene, both radiating enlightenment and crying. And of course Carcassonne, a World Unesco Heritage site, with the basilica of St. Sernin.

Abbey of Polycarpe

Both in the basilica inside the Cité and in the cathedral and churches in the new town on the left bank of the Aude River, many beautiful pictures of Mary Magdalene can be found. Further west we come to Mirepoix known for its sculptured faces on the houses lining the market square. And the cathedral of St. Maurice, with its chapel of Mary Magdalene. And a little further west the enigmatic rock-church of Vals.

Basilica St. Sernin, Carcassonne

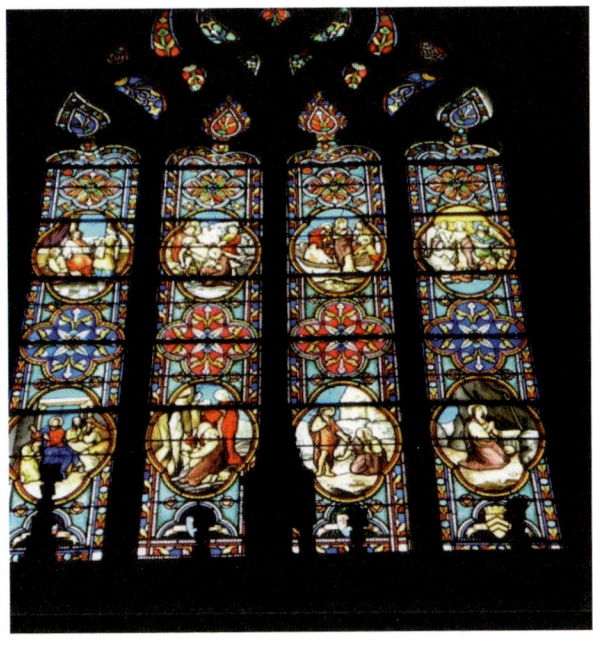

Chapel of Mary Magdalene, St. Maurice, Mirepoix

Rock-church of Vals

Then there is Foix with the St Volusien church, with a panel of the Last Supper where the person next to Jesus is clearly a woman. Pamiers also has a beautiful church and cathedral. And of course a tour of the Pays Cathare should end in Toulouse. The old capital of the counts of Toulouse, descendants of Jesus and Mary Magdalene. If you feel like it you can go further west to Lourdes, now a world famous pilgrim site. Or north to Albi with its huge pink colored basilica that looks like a castle but in this huge basilica only one small picture of Mary Magdalene can be found, high up on the ceiling. Just north of Albi is the mysterious Notre Dame de la Dreche with two beautiful statues of Black Madonna's.

Cathedral of Pamiers

Don't miss the wonderful Black Madonna's of Rocamadour. Rocamour that curious complex of church buildings situated halfway up the face of a rock.

Notre Dame de la Dreche

Albi

Rocamadour

If you want to stay a bit longer in the beautiful "heart" of France, there is much to be seen. Think of places like St Guilhem-le-Desert with its Devil's Bridge and its abbey of Gellone. Milau with its magic "floating" bridge. Or Le-Puy-en-Velay with her Notre Dame de France and her Black Madonna's.

Devils Bridge

Floating Bridge of Milau

The Cathedral of Clermont-Ferrand

Notre Dame de France

Or Clermont-Ferrand with its cathedral and Black Madonna's, and Rodez with its fortified hill, Perigueux with its impressive cathedral, Limoges with its porcelain, Cahors with its bridge and Moulins with its majestic cathedral.

Cathedral, Moulins

Further north are the cities of Autun with this lovely woman standing in a side chapel of the cathedral and this curious painting of the Eucharist.

Eucharist in Autun

Autun

And a little to the north-east the ancient city of Ferrieres en Gatinais, with its church and chapel and the Notre Dame de Bethleem is well worth a visit.

Then Poitiers and Orléans. Orléans is an old cult center of Mary Magdalene, with a huge cathedral and the magic Notre Dame des Miracles.

Notre Dame des Miracles, Orléans

The best way to finish the pilgrimage is no doubt by visiting the magic cathedral of Chartres. What a wonderful place. What a beautiful church. Entering this church feels like an initiation. Most certainly so if you walk its labyrinth, which can be done on Fridays. The cathedral has two black Madonna's, one in the crypt and one in the church itself. Beautiful.

If you go north along the coast, on your way to England or to Belgium and the Netherlands, bypassing Paris, then visit, The Notre Dame de Verdelais near Bordeaux. And, of course, the sacred stones of Carnac, in Bretagne and the basilica Notre Dame Douvres La Deliverande in Normandy. And in the same city the Notre Dame de la Fidelity with its statues and windows made of glass and its Stations of the Cross painted by a Vietnamese artist. Magic!

Notre Dame de Verdelais, near Bordeaux

Notre Dame Douvres La Deliverande

Sacred Stones of Carnac

Further north is the Notre Dame de Grace in Honfleur. You might also stop at Rouen and Amiens with their beautiful, impressive cathedrals. But as you may have seen, cathedrals are not very "Mary Magdalene friendly". They are more like "empire state churches". Huge, impressive buildings, beautiful and powerful, but cold. You won't find many statues or portraits of Mary Magdalene in those places. With, of course, a few exceptions like Aix-en-Provence and Moulins. Before going over, across or under the Channel, or leaving France for Belgium, visit the wonderful Notre Dame de Boulogne with its Black Madonna, in this case she is brown, and its huge crypts. If you are going east to Luxembourg then don't miss the beautiful church of Avioth, near the Belgium border. Also with a Black Madonna. And of course Stenay and the abbey of Orval.

Notre Dame de Grace, Honfleur

Notre Dame de Boulogne

Church of Avioth

This whole pilgrimage will take at least four weeks.

Probably more.

But they will be

Unforgettable weeks.

A MESSAGE TO THE CHURCH

Dear Church, did you know that on several occasions it were women that saved the church? That the women often persuaded their men to support Christianity. On crucial moments in time. Let me give you a few examples.

First of all it was Mary Magdalene who brought "true" Christianity from the First Holy Land to the Second Holy Land. True Christianity, or Spiritual Christianity, or Esoteric Christianity, or Gnostic Christianity. Christianity that lasted. Because she preached the good news, the true message of Christ. A message of hope, of spiritual growth, of love. A message that was cherished. A message that was kept in the hearts of the people. Despite the murderous Albigensian crusade, despite the Inquisition, despite the religious war and even despite the French revolution. A message that spread, with great success, to France and England.

Think of Anna, the daughter of Joseph of Arimathea and Enygeusa, who was married to Bran the blessed. Who spread the teachings of Jesus in England, resulting in Pelagianism and Celtic Christianity. Think of Princess Elaine, a direct descendant of Joseph and Enygeusa, later called Helena. She was the mother of Constantine who was the first emperor to allow Christianity in his Roman Empire in 313 AD.

She was also responsible for building the Holy Sepulchre Church in Jerusalem and the Catherina Cloister in the Sinai desert. Think of Clothilde, the wife of the powerful Merovingian King Clovis. Who persuaded her husband to be baptized in 496 AD in Reims, effectively saving Christianity for France or France for Christianity? Think of the French princess Bertha, who persuaded her husband, the Saxon King Ethelbert of Kent, to be baptized in 597 in Canterbury. Effectively replacing Celtic Christianity with the more "traditional", Orthodox Christianity. Including the rule of Rome.

Cloister of St. Catherina, Sinai

There are many more examples. Of female martyrs, brutally killed by the Romans. Of women burned for being a Cathar or a faudit, a person helping the Cathars. Of women tortured and killed by the Inquisition. Of women saving France, like Joan of Arc, one of the patron saints of France. Who during the Hundred Years Wars with the English freed Orléans. And made the coronation of Charles VII in Reims possible, thereby saving the King for France or France for the King.

Think of all the women suffering badly from witch-hunting. And dying for their belief in God and nature. Think of the many female saints and the women who had visions, like in Lourdes and Fatima. Women doing very important work for the Church.

Joan of Arc, Orléans

That's why I to say to the Church: "be grateful to those women. Honor them. And better still, honor all women. Embrace the Sacred Femininity. And admit women, as priestesses, to the Church."

Christianity nowadays is a long way from the Christianity that Jesus and Mary Magdalene preached. The original Christianity. Teachings, which we now would call "Gnostic". Present day Christianity is a different religion, if you can call it a religion at all. It is more like a state religion, a power tool used by emperors and popes to keep the masses under control. A religion based on fear and guilt and sin. Fear of God, fear of the Church, fear of prosecution, fear of Hell. A religion infused with the original sin. A religion where people can always be found guilty of something, especially women. The Church is no loving society that takes care of the welfare and spiritual growth of their believers. It is a harsh, impersonal, hierarchical structure. The Churches have positioned themselves between God and men. As intermediaries, speaking to God on behalf of their subjects. "Buying" places for their wealthy believers in Heaven. A Church with popes, cardinals, bishops and priests all striving for power, material wealth, personal gain, and other earthly pleasures. Where women and children were and still are, abused, right up to the present day. Watch for example the film *"The Magdalene Sisters" (2002)*. And think of all the little boys and girls abused by priests. And about the bishops and cardinals covering things up.

The Roman Catholic Church, though still powerful, is fast losing ground. Churches are closing down. Scandals plague Rome. But not only Rome. The Protestant churches suffer as well. With their rigid belief systems, their masculine superiority and their hypocrisy. Like the God-fearing, law abiding fishermen, who without any remorse exceed the fish quota. If money is involved, big money, then religious principles are easily forgotten.

Most Protestant churches are even further away from Mary Magdalene than the Catholic churches. You won't see, as far as I know, Protestant churches dedicated to Mary

Magdalene. Nor chapels, statues, or paintings of her. Many "good" Protestants consider her still a sinner, doing penitence for her deeds. And for being a woman, a beautiful woman.

Rome finally "reinstated" Mary Magdalene in 1969 and declared her officially a saint, with her feast day on July 22nd. She had, according to the Church, done enough penance! Penance for what? They didn't say. Well, let's turn things around. And ask the Church "When are you doing penance?"

Well here we are. In the 21st century. No longer afraid to speak our mind. And able to talk freely about our beliefs. Free to read forbidden books and go wherever we want. Here we are, with our incredible technological progress. And our growing spiritual awareness. Step by step exposing what the Church has done. Showing Her for what she is. An arrogant, hollow and obsolete power structure. Here we are, rudely awakened by catastrophes, volcanic eruptions, earthquakes, tidal waves, terrorist attacks, scandals, corruption, financial and economic crises. Hoping for a better world. Where we can respect each other, and Mother Earth and nature. Looking for new sets of values. And more attention for spiritual growth than for material wealth. For equality between the sexes. For "Love" as the guiding factor in our belief systems. For harmony in our lives, instead of fear, sin and guilt.

Mary Magdalene

Dear Church, may I give you some advice? On how to turn the tide? On how to win back the love and respect of your "customers, your believers?"

"Use" Mary Magdalene. "Use" that magnificent woman. Loved by men and women alike. Go back to the roots of Christianity. To what Jesus and Mary Magdalene originally preached. It is not such a big thing. You have not deviated too far from their beliefs. And besides, you have no choice. For now the painful and often terrible truth of your manipulations during the past 1,700 years is coming to light. Day after day. So see the worldwide revival of Mary Magdalene as an opportunity, a golden opportunity, presented to you in difficult times. An opportunity you cannot afford to lose. The opportunity to save the Church and change its course.

Fortunately there are promising signs. Such as the mass celebrated on July 22nd 2010 by the bishop of Narbonne and Carcassonne in the little church of Mary Magdalene in Rennes-le-Château. In his "speech" he painted a much more positive picture of Mary Magdalene and her importance for the Church and for mankind then his predecessor did in the year 2000. That speech was very traditional. And that bishop did not enjoy coming to this

The Bishop in Rennes-le-Chateau

strange, heretical church. But he had no choice. For this was the most famous church dedicated to Mary Magdalene in his bishopric. And the year was 2.000 which reads in Roman capitals "MM"!

Mary Magdalene, the "Savior" of the church! Wouldn't that be something? Mary Magdalene, the Apostle of the Apostles. Mary Magdalene, the embodiment of love and Sacred Femininity. She and all women with her are sorely missed in your Church. She is well known now, thanks to books like "*The Holy Blood and the Holy Grail*" and "*The Da Vinci Code*". She is the only person who might save the Church. The "person" who might be able to bring the people back to the Church. So open your door to Mary Magdalene. Embrace her. She might bring you the love and the wisdom you so sadly miss. Even though I fear that she herself, according to channeled information from one of my psychic "friends" has neither desire nor intent to save the Church of Rome".

Or are you waiting for the fulfillment of the prophesies of St. Malachy and Nostradamus? Prophesies that are so graphically described in the book "The Last Pope, The Decline and Fall of the Church of Rome", by John Hogue.

I hope not!

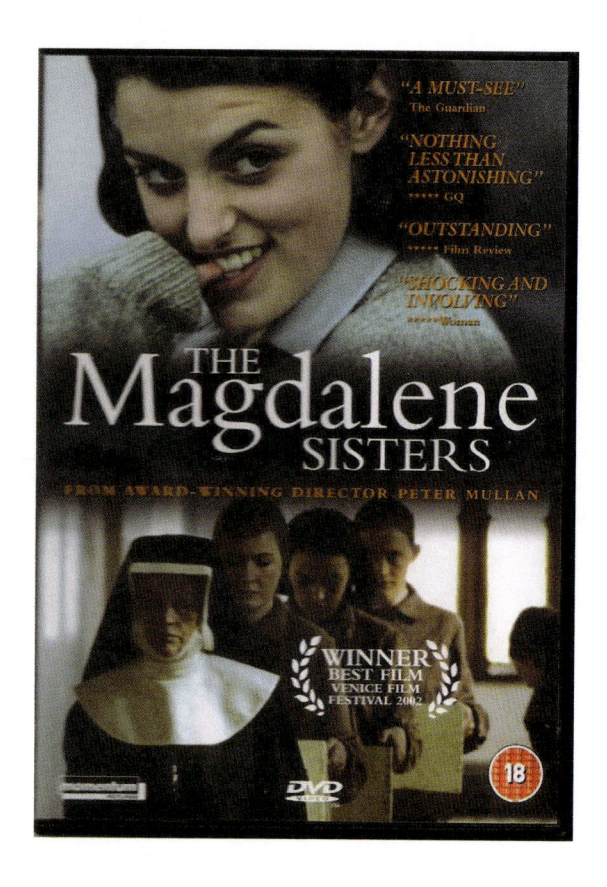

Nostradamus

EPILOGUE

Mary Magdalene is alive. Alive in the minds and hearts of millions of people, all over the world. Men and women alike. We adore her. We embrace her. We welcome her in a world so needy of her love, her compassion and her wisdom. We celebrate the new interest for the Apocrypha, the forbidden gospels, the original teachings of Jesus and Mary Magdalene, Gnostic Christianity. We welcome the return of sacred femininity, so strongly embedded in the person of Mary Magdalene. And we hope, we dearly hope, that all this will make a change. A change in this harsh, materialistic world. A world in the midst of catastrophic events. And on the verge of collapse.

Now we know more about our Christian roots. About the first Holy Country. Palestine, Judea or Israel, or whatever it is called. From the Nag Hammadi parchments, the Qumran scrolls and several other documents and manuscripts. From archeological surveys, C-14 dating, scientific research of the customs and culture of the era, from handwriting, art, symbolism, technology, gematria. We may think different from what the Church tells us. About what happened after the crucifixion. What happened to Jesus and Mary Magdalene, their journey to France. And about Joseph of Arimathea in England. And their children, the Desposyni.

We know more about Mary Magdalene in France, the Second Holy Land. Maybe not exactly where she landed, where she lived, where she preached or where she is buried. But we know about her teachings. How important, forceful and enlightening they were. How full of love and compassion. Aimed at the spiritual enlightenment of the people. Teachings of hope, growth and direct contact with God. Teachings that made an incredible impression on the people in the South of France. So much, that no force could wipe it out. No battles, no burning, no inquisition, no witch-hunt, nothing.

We know more about France, the Second Holy Land. I say "Holy" even though the reasons for embracing Roman Christianity, State Christianity, were not always Holy, or driven by religious motives. More often they were political or commercial. But the power of France was always there, very real. In the way the emperors, kings, pope and cardinals interacted. And in the way they enforced their will on the people. That was very real. So real and so harsh that only the brutal French Revolution (1789-1799) could put an end to it.

We know more about what happened in France during the past twenty centuries. How the Romans, Visigoths, Merovingian's and Carolingians acted. What their belief systems where. We know more about the early renaissance in various parts of France. About the crusades to The First Holy Land. About the Cathars and the brutal Albigensian crusade. About the Knights Templar and the secrets they brought home. About the Huguenots and the French Revolution. About the power of secret societies. And the revival of Catharism.

But most of all we know more about Mary Magdalene. In my view the most important woman of the past 2,000 years. We know her through the stories and the folktales that are told about her. We know her from her pictures. Pictures that say more than a thousand words. We know about her from books and channeled information. And we know about her from visiting "her" places. And feeling her energy. That loving, healing, warm, female energy. Through Mary Magdalene and through the many pictures of Black Madonna's we got a better view of the ancient Goddesses. And their awesome power. A better understanding of the importance of sacred femininity. And the need to harmonize our male and female energies.

The pictures of Mary Magdalene have taken us back to the roots of Gnostic Christianity. To the love, the power and the devotion of Mary Magdalene. Showing her in love with Jesus, showing her as his bride, as a pregnant woman, as the apostle of the apostles, preaching to the people. Showing her in sorrow, mourning the death of Jesus. Or consoling his mother and sisters. Showing her surprise at meeting him at the open grave. Showing her as a woman, a real woman, with all the characteristics of a woman. A wonderful woman, a beautiful woman, a total woman. A Goddess.

Thank you Mary Magdalene for allowing us to know you a little better.

BIBLIOGRAPHY

- Alford, Alan F. When the Gods came down
- Andersen, L. Shannon. The Magdalene Awakening, Symbols & Synchronicity Heralding the Re-emergence of the Divine Feminine
- Andrews, Richard and Schellenberger, Paul. The Tomb of God
- Baigent, Michael. "The Jesus Papers, Exposing the Greatest Cover-Up in History".
- Baigent, Michael; Lee, Richard; Lincoln, Henry. The Holy Blood and the Holy Grail.
- Bailey, Margaret and Nahmad, Claire. The Secret Teachings of Mary Magdalene.
- Begg, Ean. The Cult of the Black Virgin.
- Bonvin, Jaques. Vierges Noires, la réponse vient de la Terre
- Brown, Dan. The Da Vinci Code,
- Browne, Sylvia. The Two Mary's
- Burnstein, Dan and Keijzer, Arne J. Secrets of Mary Magdalene
- Doumerge, Christian. L'Epouse du Christ; La Terre Blue; L'Evangile Interdit (Ste Marie Madeleine et le Secret des Cathares)
- Gardner, Laurence. "Bloodline of the Holy Grail", 1996; " The Magdalene Legacy, The Jesus and Mary Bloodline Conspiracy", 2005, "The Serpent Grail" 2005, written together with Gary Osborn, "The Secret teachings of Mary Magdalene" 2006 and "The Grail Enigma, The hidden descent of Jesus", 2008
- Haskins, Susan. Myth and Metaphor
- Heartsong, Claire. "Anna, the grandmother of Jesus"
- Hogue, John. The Last Pope, The Decline and Fall of the Church of Rome
- Jourdaa, Frederique and Olivier Corsan. Sur les pas de Marie Madeleine, or Following in the tracks of Mary Magdalene
- Kelen, Jaqueline. Marie Madeleine ou la beauté de Dieu or Mary Magdalene or the beauty of God
- Kenyon, Tom and Sion, Judy. The Magdalen Manuscript
- Ladurie, Emmanuel Le Roy. Montaillou
- Magdalena, Flo Aeveia. I remember Union
- Malachi, Tau. St. Mary Magdalene, The Gnostic Tradition of the Holy Bride
- Markale, Jean. Cathedral of the Black Madonna; The Church of Mary Magdalene
- McOwan, Kathleen. "The expected One" and "The book of Love".
- Pagels, Elaine. Beyond Belief
- Phillips, Graham. The Chalice of Magdalene, The search for the Cup that held the blood of Christ
- Picknett, Lynn and Clive, Prince. The Templar Revelation.
- Picknett, Lynn. Mary Magdalene, Her secret lies at the heart of the Da Vinci Code
- Rabanus, Maurus (776-856), archbishop of Mainz. "The life of Mary Magdalen"
- Ralls, Karen. Maria Magdalene

- Rigby, Greg. On Earth as it is in Heaven
- Simmans, Graham. Jesus After the Crucifixion
- Starbird, Margaret. The Woman with the Alabaster Jar; The Goddess in the Gospels; Magdalene's Lost Legacy
- Strachan, Gordon. The Bible's Hidden Cosmology
- Thomas, Gordon. Magdalene, Jesus and the woman who loved him
- Voragine, Jacob de." Legenda Aurea", written between 1260-1264, describing the life's of all saints.
- Welborn, Amy. De-coding Mary Magdalene, Truth Legend, and Lies.
- Whitehouse, Maggy. The Marriage of Jesus
- Wineyard, Valery. Mary, Jesus, and the Charismatic Priest; The Visgothic Inheritance

About Jaap Rameijer

Jaap Rameijer was born in 1945 in Utrecht, the Netherlands. He served for 15 years in the Royal Netherlands Navy as a weapons engineering officer and for 10 years at Fokker Aircraft Manufacturer as a program manager for helicopters. He gained a Master degree in Law and in Business Administration. He held several high posts in Health Insurance companies, psychiatric hospitals, universities and high schools.

He is a man of two worlds. Highly interested in technology and management, but also deeply spiritual. A universal man, with his feet firmly on the ground.

After retiring to Rennes-le-Chateau in the French Pyrenees he absorbed himself in the mysteries of that magical place. His domaine called Les Labadous has been converted into a spiritual centre. People from all over the world come to this place.

Nowadays he is hosting tours, writing books, coaching people and giving presentations. He wrote books and articles about Rennes-le-Chateau, Glastonbury, the Cathars, Orbs and Mary Magdalene. But also books about the relationship between men and women and the pleasure of cooking natural food.

Jaap has a keen sense of humor. He loves to bring people and ideas together and help them grow spiritually.

Books by Jaap Rameijer

Made in the USA
San Bernardino, CA
28 August 2014